100 KNITTED TILES

Charts and patterns for knitted motifs inspired by decorative tiles

EDITED BY SARAH CALLARD

DAVID & CHARLES

www.davidandcharles.com

CONTENTS

HOW TO USE THIS BOOK

This collection of 100 beautiful knitted designs features patterns inspired by decorative ceramic tiles from around the world. You can use these designs to create your own projects, such as blankets or cushions – or try one of the five exciting projects, which show you other ways in which the tiles could be assembled. Let these inspire you to create your own projects and take the chance to try new techniques and experiment with different colour combinations.

Each tile has instructions to follow to complete the design. Many of the colourwork patterns are worked from a chart. Some of the texture and lace tiles also have a chart. You will need to read the instructions to understand when to work the chart or how many repeats to work (see Techniques: Reading Charts).

All of the tiles and projects in this book have been designed with Scheepjes Metropolis yarn – a versatile fingering weight (4ply) yarn with a classic fibre blend of 75% extrafine Merino wool and 25% nylon. Metropolis has enough definition to handle cables and colourwork but also blocks beautifully in lace and textured projects. Named after worldwide cities, the yarn is available in 80 colours, making it the perfect choice for any of these tiles and projects you choose to knit.

The publisher would like to thank Scheepjes for supplying the yarn for the tiles and projects in this book.

BASIC KIT

For most tiles, all you will need are knitting needles and yarn, plus a yarn/tapestry needle for weaving in ends. For some techniques you may need additional notions, such as a cable needle, stitch markers, beads or a crochet hook. Most tiles only need small amounts of each colour, so they are a great stash-buster. The projects specify the yarn amounts needed, and any other supplies required to complete the item.

US/UK TERMINOLOGY

Some knitting terms differ between the US and UK. Here is a quick guide for some of the most commonly used in this book.

US TERM	UK TERM
bind off	cast off
fingering weight yarn	4ply yarn
gauge	tension
seed stitch	moss stitch
stockinette stitch	stocking stitch

KNITTING NEEDLE SIZES

In order to achieve the finished size listed in the pattern, you should work to the gauge (tension) provided with each tile or project. Everyone knits differently, so you may find you need to adjust the needle size up or down to achieve the correct gauge. This table shows size conversions between US, metric or UK standards, starting from smallest needle size to largest.

US	METRIC	UK
1	2.25mm	13
1.5	2.5mm	13 or 12
2	2.75mm	12
2.5	3mm	11
3	3.25mm	10
4	3.5mm	10 or 9
5	3.75mm	9
6	4mm	8
7	4.5mm	7
8	5mm	6

ABBREVIATIONS

BOR – beginning of round

CC – contrast colour

cdd – central double decrease

DPN(s) – double pointed needle(s)

garter stitch – when working flat, knit all rows; in the round, alternate knit and purl rounds

k – knit

kfb – knit front and back of same stitch

LH – left-hand

m1L – make 1 stitch left

m1R – make 1 stitch right

MC – main colour

p – purl

psso – pass slip stitch over

rep – repeat

RH – right-hand

RS – right side

seed (moss) stitch – alternate knits and purls every stitch and every row/round

sk2p – slip 1 knitwise, k2tog, pass slipped stitch over

skpo – slip 1 knitwise, knit 1, pass slipped stitch over

ssk – slip 2 stitches knitwise one at a time, knit these 2 stitches together through the back loop

st(s) – stitch(es)

stockinette (stocking) stitch – when working flat, knit on right side rows and purl on wrong side rows; in the round, knit all rounds

tbl – through the back loop(s)

tog – together, knitting or purling as many stitches together as given

WS – wrong side

yo – yarn over

* or ** – repeat instructions following asterisk(s) as directed

[ ] – work instructions within brackets as many times stated

Some tiles have special abbreviations used for their patterns. These are listed with the individual tile patterns.

THE
TILES

GEOMETRIC FLOWERS

DESIGNER: CARMEN JORISSEN

YARN

A - Teal (Suwon 018)

B - Brick Red (Lagos 042)

NEEDLES

US size 2.5 (3mm) needles, or as needed to achieve gauge (tension)

GAUGE (TENSION)

31 sts x 30 rows = 4 x 4in (10 x 10cm) square

FINISHED SIZE

5¾ x 5¾in (14.5 x 14.5cm)

KEY

☐	RS: knit WS: purl
▨	A
■	B

NOTES

This tile is worked in stockinette (stocking) stitch following the colourwork chart. The colour not in use should be stranded loosely across the back of the colour being used (see Techniques: Stranded Colourwork).

To make your colourwork look neat, wrap yarn B at the start of every row, preferably on the second stitch, as follows:

On RS rows, insert RH needle into next stitch (to be worked in yarn A), lay yarn B horizontally from right to left over RH needle, knit the stitch using yarn A. Yarn B is now wrapped. Make sure yarn B is not being pulled through the stitch.

On WS rows, insert RH needle into next stitch (to be worked in yarn A), hold yarn B up so that it lays vertically across RH needle, purl the stitch using yarn A.

PATTERN

Using yarn A, cast on 44 sts.

Set-Up Row (WS): Using yarn A, purl to end.

Join in yarn B.

Work Rows 1 to 41 of chart.

Cut yarn B.

Next Row (WS): Using yarn A, purl to end.

Bind (cast) off all sts.

Weave in ends and block to finished size.

PINWHEEL

DESIGNER: SYLVIA WATTS-CHERRY

YARN

A - Pink (Montreal 059)

B - Teal (Suwon 018)

C - Light Blue (Lahore 014)

D - Indigo Blue (Dallas 003)

E - Yellow (Brasov 038)

F - Medium Blue (Washington 013)

NEEDLES

US size 1.5 (2.5mm) needles, or as needed to achieve gauge (tension)

GAUGE (TENSION)

28 sts x 56 rows = 4 x 4in (10 x 10cm) square

FINISHED SIZE

6 x 6in (15 x 15cm)

NOTES

This tile is worked in garter stitch using intarsia (see Techniques: Intarsia), with each block of colour knit from a separate ball or bobbin of yarn. Twist the yarn about to be used around the colour just used to link yarns together on WS to avoid a hole.

PATTERN

Using cable cast-on method (see Techniques: Cable Cast On), cast on 22 sts using yarn B, make a loop with yarn A and place on LH needle next to last st of yarn B. Insert RH needle into last st of yarn B and pass it over the loop of yarn A and off needle. Continue casting on 20 more sts in yarn A. 42 sts

Work Rows 1 to 84 of chart, joining in and changing colours as indicated.

Bind (cast) off all sts in pattern as follows: *bind (cast) off to 1 st before colour change, twist yarns at back and work next st with new colour, continue binding (casting) off until 1 st before next colour change; rep from * to last st.

Fasten off, pulling yarn through last st.

Weave in ends, closing any gaps with yarn tails at colour changes, and block to finished size.

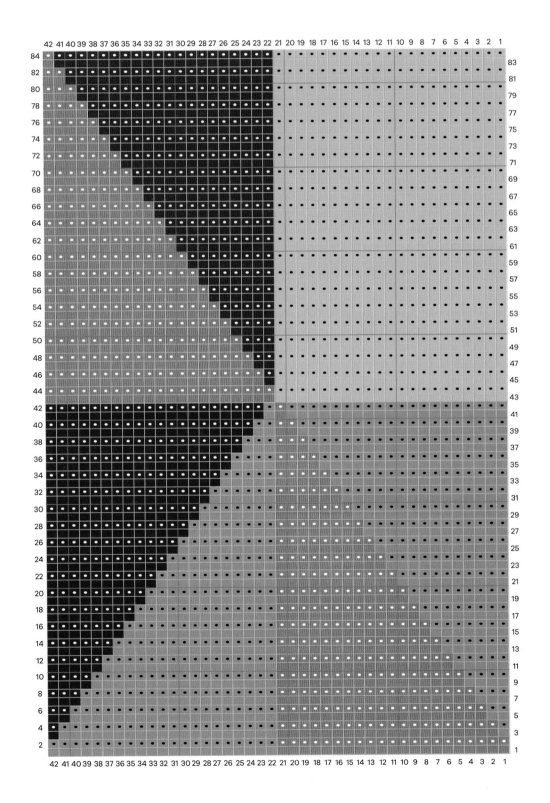

KEY

☐	RS: knit
⊡	WS: knit
▦	A
▨	B
▩	C
■	D
▤	E
■	F

ARTISAN MARVEL

DESIGNER: ASHLEIGH WEMPE

YARN

A - Medium Orange (Sevilla 076)

B - Dark Orange (Mexico City 075)

C - Light Grey (Cota 024)

D - Navy Blue (Philadelphia 007)

NEEDLES

US size 8 (5mm) DPNs

US size 7 (4.5mm) DPNs, or as needed to achieve gauge (tension)

ACCESSORIES

4 stitch markers, including one distinct for BOR

GAUGE (TENSION)

15 sts x 27 rounds = 4 x 4in (10 x 10cm) square using yarn held double on US size 7 (4.5mm) needles

FINISHED SIZE

7 x 7in (18 x 18cm)

NOTES

This tile is worked in the round from the outer edge to the centre. The yarn is held double throughout. Use two separate balls or find both ends of the ball. There is no border and the stockinette (stocking) stitch fabric will tend to roll even after blocking, so this design is intended to be part of a larger project.

When working the chart, the colour not in use should be stranded loosely across the back of the colour being used (see Techniques: Stranded Colourwork).

PATTERN

Using US size 8 (5mm) DPNs, and with one strand of yarn A and one strand of yarn B held together, cast on 108 sts. Join to work in the round, being careful not to twist the sts.

Cut yarns A and B.

Change to US size 7 (4.5mm) DPNs.

Using two strands of yarn C as MC and two strands of yarn D as CC, work as follows:

Round 1: [Work Row 1 of chart, place marker] four times, with final marker for BOR.

Continue working as set, slipping markers and working decreases as shown, until chart is complete. 12 sts

Cut all yarn strands and thread MC tail through remaining sts, pulling tight to close the hole.

Weave in ends and block to finished size.

KEY

☐	knit
╱	k2tog
╲	ssk
☐	MC
■	CC

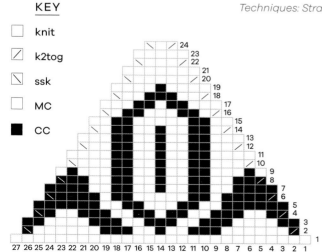

TWO MOONS

DESIGNER: ANNI HOWARD

YARN

A - Orange (Quebec 077)

B - Cream (Lyon 078)

NEEDLES

US size 3 (3.25mm) needles, or as
needed to achieve gauge (tension)

GAUGE (TENSION)

34 sts x 64 rows = 4 x 4in (10 x 10cm) square

FINISHED SIZE

6 x 6in (15 x 15cm)

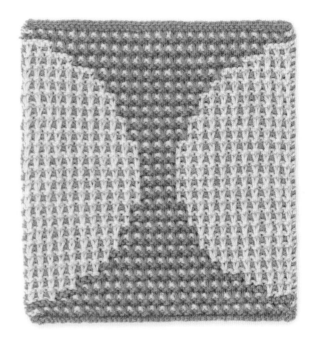

KEY

■ A

□ B

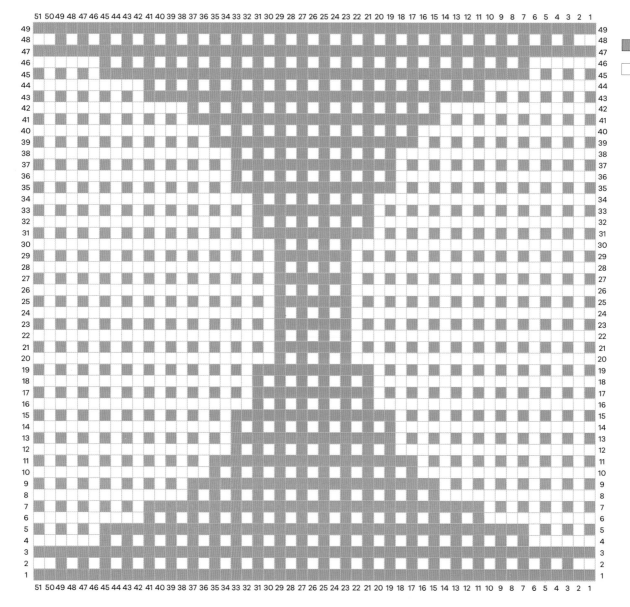

NOTES

Work this tile using mosaic knitting (see Techniques: Mosaic Knitting). Each chart row represents one RS row and one WS row. Knit stitches that are the colour of the first stitch of the row, and slip the other colour.

PATTERN

Using yarn A, cast on 51 sts.

Work from chart as follows:

Row 1 (RS): Using yarn A, knit to end.

Row 1 (WS): Using yarn A, knit to end.

Row 2 (RS): Using yarn B, k2, *slip 1 purlwise, k1; rep from * to last st, k1.

Row 2 (WS): Using yarn B, k2, *move yarn to front, slip 1 purlwise, move yarn to back, k1; rep from * to last st, k1.

Continue working from chart until Row 49 WS has been completed.

Bind (cast) off all sts knitwise using yarn A.

Weave in ends and block to finished size.

TRELLIS

DESIGNER: LYNNE ROWE

YARN

Green (Salvador 029)

NEEDLES

US size 2.5 (3mm) needles, or as needed to achieve gauge (tension)

GAUGE (TENSION)

30 sts x 42 rows = 4 x 4in (10 x 10cm) square

FINISHED SIZE

6 x 6in (15 x 15cm)

NOTES

Knit and purl stitches create a textured pattern.

PATTERN

Cast on 44 sts.

Row 1 (WS): Purl.

Row 2: K3, [p2, k10] three times, p2, k3.

Row 3: P3, [k2, p10] three times, k2, p3.

Row 4: K1, [p2, k2, p2, k6] three times, p2, k2, p2, k1.

Row 5: P1, [k2, p2, k2, p6] three times, k2, p2, k2, p1.

Row 6: P1, [k6, p2, k2, p2] three times, k6, p1.

Row 7: K1, [p6, k2, p2, k2] three times, p6, k1.

Row 8: K9, [p2, k10] twice, p2, k9.

Row 9: P9, [k2, p10] twice, k2, p9.

Rows 10 and 11: Rep Rows 6 and 7.

Rows 12 and 13: Rep Rows 4 and 5.

Rows 14 and 15: Rep Rows 2 and 3.

Rows 16 to 63: Rep Rows 4 to 15 four times.

Row 64 (RS): Knit.

Bind (cast) off all sts.

Weave in ends and block to finished size.

PERSEPHONE

DESIGNER: KARIE WESTERMANN

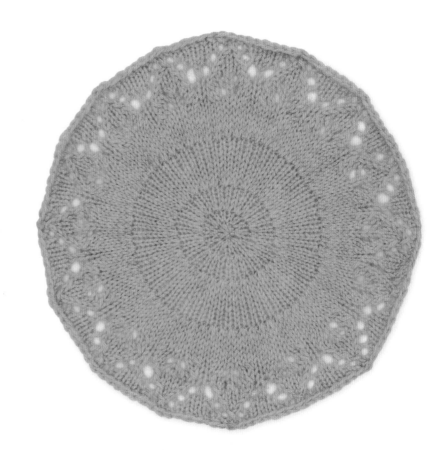

YARN

Yellow (Dhaka 040)

NEEDLES

US size 6 (4mm) DPNs, or as
needed to achieve gauge (tension)

ACCESSORIES

Stitch markers, including one distinct
for BOR

GAUGE (TENSION)

19.5 sts x 35 rounds = 4 x 4in (10 x 10cm)
square

FINISHED SIZE

8¼in (21cm) diameter

NOTES

*This circular tile is worked in the round
from the centre out.*

*Rounds 1 to 10 are also shown in the
chart, which is worked 16 times in each
round. Use stitch markers between
repeats if you prefer.*

PATTERN

Cast on 8 sts leaving a long tail. Join to
work in the round being careful not to
twist stitches. Mark the beginning of the
round.

Knit one round.

Next Round: [Kfb] eight times. 16 sts

Knit two rounds.

Next Round: *Kfb; rep from * to end.
32 sts

Knit four rounds.

Next Round: *Kfb; rep from * to end.
64 sts

Knit eight rounds.

Next Round: *Kfb; rep from * to end.
128 sts

Knit six rounds.

Round 1: *K1, k2tog, [k1, yo] twice, k1,
k2tog tbl; rep from * to end.

Round 2: Knit.

Rounds 3 and 4: Rep Rounds 1 and 2.

Round 5: *K1, yo, k2tog tbl, k3, k2tog, yo;
rep from * to end.

Round 6: Knit.

Round 7: *K2, yo, k2tog tbl, k1, k2tog, yo,
k1; rep from * to end.

Round 8: Knit.

Round 9: *K3, yo, sk2p, yo, k2; rep from *
to end.

Round 10: Knit.

Bind (cast) off using a stretchy method
as follows: k2, *slip both sts back to LH
needle, k2tog tbl, k1; rep from * to end.

Fasten off, pulling yarn through last st.

Use the cast-on yarn tail to close the
hole at the centre if needed. Weave in
ends and block to finished size.

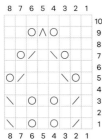
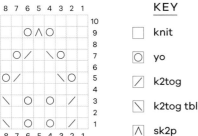

KEY

☐	knit
◯	yo
╱	k2tog
╲	k2tog tbl
⋀	sk2p

BLINKING

· · · · · · · · · · · · · · ·

DESIGNER: LILY LANGMAN

YARN

A - Teal Green (Pasay 022)

B - Cream (Lyon 078)

C - Yellow (Brasov 038)

D - Dark Green (Karachi 016)

NEEDLES

US size 1.5 (2.5mm) needles, or as
needed to achieve gauge (tension)

GAUGE (TENSION)

29 sts x 45 rows = 4 x 4in (10 x 10cm) square

FINISHED SIZE

6¼ x 5¾in (16 x 14.5cm)

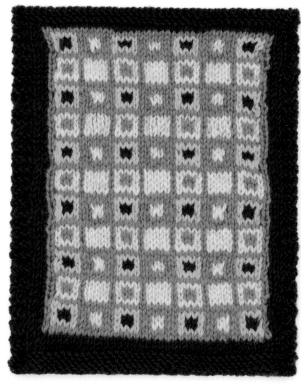

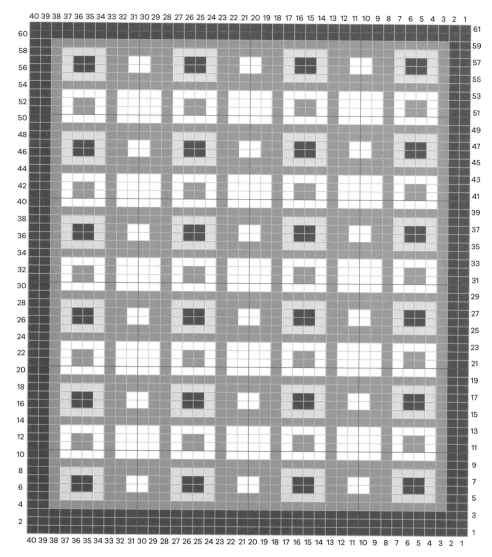

KEY

☐ RS: knit
WS: purl

▨ A

☐ B

▨ C

▨ D

NOTES

This tile is knitted with a border of garter stitch on the top and bottom edges and 3 garter stitches on each side. The chart is worked in stockinette (stocking) stitch.

When working with two or three colours at once, the colours not in use should be stranded loosely across the back of the colour being used (see Techniques: Stranded Colourwork).

When stranding the yarn becomes difficult, use a separate ball of yarn for each colour and twist the yarn about to be used around the colour just used to link yarns together on WS to avoid a hole (see Techniques: Intarsia).

If you prefer to work a smaller tile without the border, cast on 40 stitches using yarn D, work the chart, then bind (cast) off using yarn D.

PATTERN

Using yarn D, cast on 46 sts.

Work 4 rows of garter stitch.

Join in other colours as needed and work as follows:

Row 1 (RS): K3 using yarn D, knit Row 1 of chart, k3 using yarn D.

Row 2: K3 using yarn D, purl Row 2 of chart, k3 using yarn D.

Keeping first 3 sts and last 3 sts in garter stitch using yarn D throughout, continue until chart is complete.

Cut all colours except yarn D.

Work 3 rows of garter stitch.

Bind (cast) off all sts.

Weave in ends and block to finished size.

COFFEE BEAN

DESIGNER: LISA MCFETRIDGE

YARN
A - Purple (Santiago 053)
B - Pale Lavender (Taipei 006)

NEEDLES
US size 2 (2.75mm) needles, or as needed to achieve gauge (tension)

GAUGE (TENSION)
34 sts x 38 rows = 4 x 4in (10 x 10cm) square

FINISHED SIZE
6¼ x 6in (16 x 15cm)

NOTES

Strand the colour not in use loosely across the back of the colour being used (see Techniques: Stranded Colourwork).

Knit the first and last stitch of every row whether on a RS or WS row, in order to create a tight edge.

PATTERN

Using yarn A, cast on 53 sts in [k1, p1] rib using cable cast on (see Techniques: Cable Cast On).

Join in yarn B as needed.

Work Rows 1 to 57 of chart.

Bind (cast) off all sts firmly in [k1, p1] rib using yarn A.

Weave in ends and block to finished size.

KEY

	RS: knit WS: purl
•	WS: knit
■	A
□	B

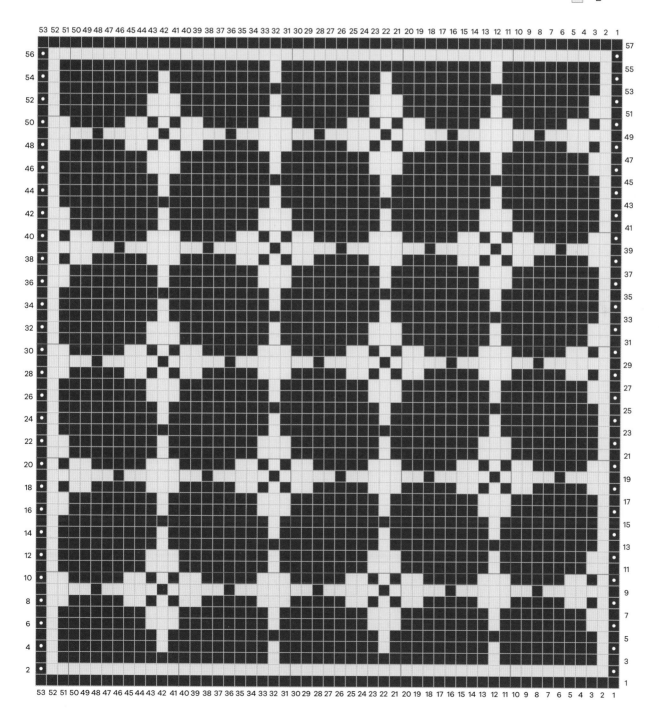

FERN LEAF

DESIGNER: KAROLINA ADAMCZYK

YARN

A - Dark Teal (Multan 017)

B - Light Teal (Marseille 019)

NEEDLES

US size 1.5 (2.5mm) DPNs, or as needed to achieve gauge (tension)

ACCESSORIES

4 stitch markers, including one distinct for BOR

GAUGE (TENSION)

29 sts x 38 rounds = 4 x 4in (10 x 10cm) square

FINISHED SIZE

6½ x 6½in (16.5 x 16.5cm)

NOTES

This tile is worked in the round from the outer edge to the centre. It begins with a ribbed border, with markers indicating the corners of the square where decreases shape the work.

The chart is repeated four times in each round. When working the chart, the colour not in use should be stranded loosely across the back of the colour being used (see Techniques: Stranded Colourwork).

PATTERN

Using yarn A, cast on 180 sts. Join to work in the round, being careful not to twist the sts.

Round 1: *[K1, p1] 22 times, k1, place marker; rep from * three more times, with the final marker for BOR.

Round 2: *Ssk, [k1, p1] 20 times, k1, k2tog, slip marker; rep from * three more times. 172 sts

Round 3: *K1, [k1, p1] 20 times, k2, slip marker; rep from * three more times.

Round 4: *Ssk, knit to 2 sts before marker, k2tog, slip marker; rep from * three more times. 164 sts

Join in yarn B.

Repeating chart four times in each round, work Rows 1 to 25 of chart, decreasing before and after markers on rounds as indicated. 28 sts

Cut yarn B and continue with yarn A only.

Next Round: Knit.

Next Round: [K2tog] 14 times, removing all markers. 14 sts

Cut yarn A and thread end through remaining sts, pulling tight to close the hole.

Weave in ends and block to finished size.

KEY

☐ knit

◣ ssk

◢ k2tog

■ A

▨ B

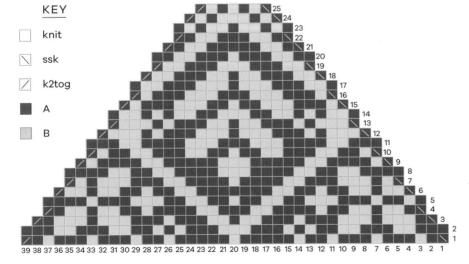

VICTORIAN DIAMONDS

DESIGNER: HELEN BIRCH

YARN

A - Cream (Lyon 078)

B - Orange (Tripoli 074)

C - Blue (Boston 011)

D - Red (Naples 043)

NEEDLES

US size 2.5 (3mm) needles, or as needed to achieve gauge (tension)

GAUGE (TENSION)

29 sts x 40 rows = 4 x 4in (10 x 10cm) square

FINISHED SIZE

6¼ x 6½in (16 x 16.5cm)

KEY

☐	RS: knit / WS: purl
•	RS: purl / WS: knit
☐	A
	B
	C
	D

NOTES

This design works the seed (moss) stitch border as part of the motif.

When working with two or three colours at once, the colours not in use should be stranded loosely across the back of the colour being used (see Techniques: Stranded Colourwork).

When stranding the yarn becomes difficult, use a separate ball of yarn for each colour and twist the yarn about to be used around the colour just used to link yarns together on WS to avoid a hole (see Techniques: Intarsia).

PATTERN

Using yarn A, cast on 45 sts.

Join in other colours as needed.

Work Rows 1 to 63 of chart.

Bind (cast) off all sts using yarn A.

Weave in ends and block to finished size.

STANDARD

DESIGNER: ASHLEIGH WEMPE

YARN

A – Medium Orange (Sevilla 076)

B – Dark Orange (Mexico City 075)

NEEDLES

US size 8 (5mm) DPNs, or as needed to achieve gauge (tension)

ACCESSORIES

4 stitch markers, including one distinct for BOR

GAUGE (TENSION)

15 sts x 27 rounds = 4 x 4in (10 x 10cm) square using yarn held double

FINISHED SIZE

7 x 7in (18 x 18cm)

NOTES

This tile is worked in the round from the outer edge to the centre. The yarn is held double throughout. Use two separate balls or find both ends of the ball. There is no border and the stockinette (stocking) stitch fabric will tend to roll even after blocking, so this design is intended to be part of a larger project.

PATTERN

Using one strand of yarn A and one strand of yarn B held together, cast on 108 sts. Join to work in the round, being careful not to twist the sts.

Round 1: [K27, place marker] four times, with final marker for BOR.

Round 2: [K2tog, knit to 2 sts before marker, ssk, slip marker] four times. 8 sts decreased

Round 3: Knit.

Rep Rounds 2 to 3 until 20 sts remain, then rep only Round 2 once more. 12 sts

Cut yarn and thread tail through remaining sts, pulling tight to close the hole.

Weave in ends and block to finished size.

FACETTED

DESIGNER: LYNNE ROWE

YARN

A - Grey (Munich 079)

B - Cream (Lyon 078)

C - Black (Hamburg 080)

NEEDLES

US size 2.5 (3mm) needles, or as needed to achieve gauge (tension)

ACCESSORIES

82 iridescent seed beads, size 8/0

US size 12/6 (1mm) crochet hook for beading

GAUGE (TENSION)

30 sts x 43 rows = 4 x 4in (10 x 10cm) square measured over stockinette (stocking) stitch

FINISHED SIZE

6 x 6in (15 x 15cm)

NOTES

The centre square is worked with beadwork on blocks of colour, then borders are picked up and worked in seed (moss) stitch.

For placing beads, a crochet hook is used to place the beads on the sts as the rows are knitted. Make sure your crochet hook is small enough to go through the beads.

Place bead as follows: Knit to position of next bead placement. Put a bead on the shaft of the crochet hook. Remove the next stitch from LH needle using the hook, positioning the stitch above the bead. Carefully pull the stitch through the bead by sliding the bead up and off the hook so that the bead sits on the base of the stitch. Replace the stitch on the LH needle and knit the stitch.

PATTERN

CENTRE SQUARE

Using yarn A, cast on 31 sts.

Row 1 (RS): Knit.

Row 2: Purl.

Row 3: [K3, place bead] seven times, k3.

Row 4: Purl.

Row 5: K5, place bead, [k3, place bead] five times, k5.

Row 6: Purl.

Rows 7 to 10: Rep Rows 3 to 6.

Rows 11 and 12: Rep Rows 3 and 4.

Row 13: Knit.

Change to yarn B.

Row 14 and following WS rows to Row 32: Purl.

Row 15: Knit.

Row 17: K15, place bead, k15.

Row 19: K14, place bead, k1, place bead, k14.

Row 21: K13, [place bead, k1] twice, place bead, k13.

Row 23: K12, [place bead, k1] three times, place bead, k12.

Row 25: Rep Row 21.

Row 27: Rep Row 19.

Row 29: Rep Row 17.

Row 31: Knit.

Row 33: Knit.

Change to yarn A.

Rows 34 to 44: Rep Rows 2 to 12.

Bind (cast) off all sts.

BOTTOM BORDER

With RS facing and using yarn C, pick up and knit 31 sts along cast-on edge.

Row 1: K1, *p1, k1; rep from * to end.

Rep Row 1 seven more times.

Bind (cast) off all sts.

TOP BORDER

Work as for Bottom Border along bound-off (cast-off) edge.

SIDE BORDERS (BOTH ALIKE)

With RS facing and using yarn C, pick up and knit 6 sts along side edge of top/bottom border, then pick up and knit 31 sts along centre square edge, and finally pick up and knit 6 sts along side edge of bottom/top border. 43 sts

Row 1: K1, *p1, k1; rep from * to end.

Rep Row 1 seven more times.

Bind (cast) off all sts.

FINISHING

Weave in ends and block to finished size.

NORDIC HEARTS

DESIGNER: KARIE WESTERMANN

YARN

A - Cream (Toulouse 030)

B - Red (Milan 057)

NEEDLES

US size 2 (2.75mm) DPNs, or as needed to achieve gauge (tension)

ACCESSORIES

4 stitch markers, including one distinct for BOR

GAUGE (TENSION)

24 sts x 42 rounds = 4 x 4in (10 x 10cm) square

FINISHED SIZE

7 x 7in (18 x 18cm)

NOTES

This tile is worked in the round from the outer edge to the centre in stockinette (stocking) stitch (every round knit).

When working the chart, the colour not in use should be stranded loosely across the back of the colour being used (see Techniques: Stranded Colourwork).

PATTERN

Using yarn A, cast on 176 sts. Join to work in the round, being careful not to twist the sts.

Knit 1 round.

Purl 1 round.

Next Round: *K44, place marker; rep from * three more times, with the final marker for BOR.

Next Round: *P1, p2tog, p39, p2tog tbl, slip marker; rep from * three more times. 168 sts

Join in yarn B.

Repeating chart four times in each round, work Rows 1 to 38 of chart, decreasing before and after markers on rounds as indicated. 16 sts

Cut yarn A and continue with yarn B only.

Next Round: [K2tog] eight times, removing all markers. 8 sts

Cut yarn B and thread end through remaining sts, pulling tight to close the hole.

Weave in ends and block to finished size.

KEY

- ☐ knit
- ╱ k2tog
- ╲ ssk
- ☐ A
- ■ B

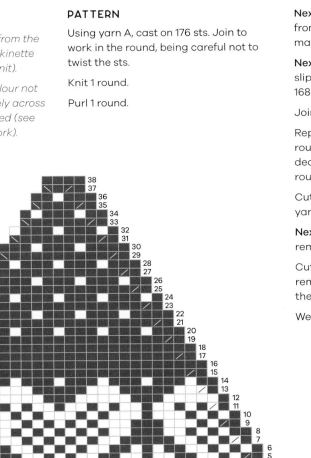

TREILLAGE

DESIGNER: JACQUI GOULBOURN

YARN
Pink (Montreal 059)

NEEDLES
US size 2 (2.75mm) needles, or as needed to achieve gauge (tension)

ACCESSORIES
Cable needle

GAUGE (TENSION)
31 sts x 43 rows = 4 x 4in (10 x 10cm) square

FINISHED SIZE
6 x 6in (15 x 15cm)

NOTES
Cables are worked over 2, 3 or 5 stitches, defined in Special Abbreviations. Rows 1 to 65 are also shown in the chart.

SPECIAL ABBREVIATIONS

1/1 LC: 1 over 1 left cross – slip 1 st to cable needle, hold at front of work, k1 from LH needle, k1 from cable needle

1/1 RC: 1 over 1 right cross – slip 1 st to cable needle, hold at back of work, k1 from LH needle, k1 from cable needle

1/1 LPC: 1 over 1 left cross with purl – slip 1 st to cable needle, hold at front of work, p1 from LH needle, k1 from cable needle

1/1 RPC: 1 over 1 right cross with purl – slip 1 st to cable needle, hold at back of work, k1 from LH needle, p1 from cable needle

2/1 LC: 2 over 1 left cross – slip 2 sts to cable needle, hold at front of work, k1 from LH needle, k2 from cable needle

2/1 RC: 2 over 1 right cross – slip 1 st to cable needle, hold at back of work, k2 from LH needle, k1 from cable needle

2/1 LPC: 2 over 1 left cross with purl – slip 2 sts to cable needle, hold at front of work, p1 from LH needle, k2 from cable needle

2/1 RPC: 2 over 1 right cross with purl – slip 1 st to cable needle, hold at back of work, k2 from LH needle, p1 from cable needle

1/1/1 RPC: 1 over 1 over 1 right cross with purl – slip 2 sts to cable needle, hold at back of work, k1 from LH needle, slip left-most st from cable needle to LH needle, hold cable needle with remaining st at front of work, p1 from LH needle, k1 from cable needle

2/1/2 RPC: 2 over 2 over 1 right cross with purl – slip 3 sts to cable needle, hold at back of work, k2 from LH needle, slip left-most st from cable needle to LH needle, hold cable needle with remaining 2 sts at front of work, p1 from LH needle, k2 from cable needle

PATTERN

Cast on 47 sts.

Row 1 (RS): Knit.

Row 2: P1, k45, p1.

Row 3: K1, p1, k43, p1, k1.

Row 4: P1, k1, p43, k1, p1.

Row 5: K1, p1, k2, p3, 2/1 LPC, p2, k2, p2, 1/1 RPC, 1/1 LPC, p2, k3, p2, 1/1 RPC, 1/1 LPC, p2, k2, p2, 2/1 RPC, p3, k2, p1, k1.

Row 6: P1, k1, p2, k4, [p2, k2] twice, [p1, k2] twice, p3, [k2, p1] twice, [k2, p2] twice, k4, p2, k1, p1.

Row 7: K1, p1, k2, p4, 2/1 LPC, p4, 1/1 RPC, p2, 1/1 LPC, p2, k1, p2, 1/1 RPC, p2, 1/1 LPC, p4, 2/1 RPC, p4, k2, p1, k1.

Row 8: P1, k1, p2, k5, p2, [k4, p1] twice, [k2, p1] twice, k4, p1, k4, p2, k5, p2, k1, p1.

Row 9: K1, p1, k2, p5, 2/1 LPC, p2, 1/1 RPC, p4, 1/1 LPC, p3, 1/1 RPC, p4, 1/1 LPC, p2, 2/1 RPC, p5, k2, p1, k1.

Row 10: P1, k1, p2, k6, p2, k2, p1, k6, p1, k3, p1, k6, p1, k2, p2, k6, p2, k1, p1.

Row 11: K1, p1, k7, p1, 2/1 LPC, 1/1 RPC, p1, k4, p1, 1/1 LPC, p1, 1/1 RPC, p1, k4, p1, 1/1 LPC, 2/1 RPC, p1, k7, p1, k1.

Row 12: P1, k1, p7, k2, p3, k2, p4, k2, p1, k1, p1, k2, p4, k2, p3, k2, p7, k1, p1.

Row 13: K1, p1, k3, yo, ssk, k2tog, yo, p2, 2/1 LC, p2, yo, ssk, k2tog, yo, p2, 1/1/1 RPC, p2, yo, ssk, k2tog, yo, p2, 2/1 RC, p2, yo, ssk, k2tog, yo, k3, p1, k1.

Row 14: Rep Row 12.

Row 15: K1, p1, k7, p1, 1/1 RPC, 2/1 LPC, p1, k4, p1, 1/1 RPC, p1, 1/1 LPC, p1, k4, p1, 2/1 RPC, 1/1 LPC, p1, k7, p1, k1.

Row 16: P1, k1, p2, k6, p1, k2, p2, k6, p1, k3, p1, k6, p2, k2, p1, k6, p2, k1, p1.

Row 17: K1, p1, k2, p5, 1/1 RPC, p2, 2/1 LPC, p4, 1/1 RPC, p3, 1/1 LPC, p4, 2/1 RPC, p2, 1/1 LPC, p5, k2, p1, k1.

Row 18: P1, k1, p2, [k5, p1, k4, p2, k4, p1] twice, k5, p2, k1, p1.

Row 19: K1, p1, k2, p4, 1/1 RPC, p4, 2/1 LPC, p2, 1/1 RPC, p5, 1/1 LPC, p2, 2/1 RPC, p4, 1/1 LPC, p4, k2, p1, k1.

Row 20: P1, k1, p2, k4, p1, k6, p2, k2, p1, k1, p5, k1, p1, k2, p2, k6, p1, k4, p2, k1, p1.

Row 21: K1, p1, k2, p3, 1/1 RPC, p1, k4, p1, 2/1 LPC, 1/1 RPC, p1, k1, yo, cdd, yo, k1, p1, 1/1 LPC, 2/1 RPC, p1, k4, p1, 1/1 LPC, p3, k2, p1, k1.

Row 22: P1, k1, p2, k3, p1, k2, p4, k2, p3, k2, p5, k2, p3, k2, p4, k2, p1, k3, p2, k1, p1.

Row 23: K1, p1, k2, p3, k1, p2, yo, ssk, k2tog, yo, p2, 2/1 LC, p2, k1, yo, cdd, yo, k1, p2, 2/1 RC, p2, yo, ssk, k2tog, yo, p2, k1, p3, k2, p1, k1.

Row 24: Rep Row 22.

Row 25: K1, p1, k2, p3, 1/1 LPC, p1, k4, p1, 1/1 RPC, 2/1 LPC, p1, k1, yo, cdd, yo, k1, p1, 2/1 RPC, 1/1 LPC, p1, k4, p1, 1/1 RPC, p3, k2, p1, k1.

Row 26: P1, k1, p2, k4, p1, k6, p1, k2, p2, k1, p5, k1, p2, k2, p1, k6, p1, k4, p2, k1, p1.

Row 27: K1, p1, k2, p4, 1/1 LPC, p4, 1/1 RPC, p2, 2/1 LPC, p5, 2/1 RPC, p2, 1/1 LPC, p4, 1/1 RPC, p4, k2, p1, k1.

Row 28: P1, k1, p2, k5, [p1, k4] twice, p2, k5, p2, [k4, p1] twice, k5, p2, k1, p1.

Row 29: K1, p1, k2, p5, 1/1 LPC, p2, 1/1 RPC, p4, 2/1 LPC, p3, 2/1 RPC, p4, 1/1 LPC, p2, 1/1 RPC, p5, k2, p1, k1.

Row 30: P1, k1, p2, k6, p1, k2, p1, k6, p2, k3, p2, k6, p1, k2, p1, k6, p2, k1, p1.

Row 31: K1, p1, k6, p2, 1/1 LPC, 1/1 RPC, p1, k4, p1, 2/1 LPC, p1, 2/1 RPC, p1, k4, p1, 1/1 LPC, 1/1 RPC, p2, k6, p1, k1.

Row 32: P1, k1, p6, k3, p2, k2, p4, k2, p2, k1, p2, k2, p4, k2, p2, k3, p6, k1, p1.

Row 33: K1, p1, k2, yo, ssk, k2tog, yo, p3, 1/1 LC, p2, yo, ssk, k2tog, yo, p2, 2/1/2 RPC, p2, yo, ssk, k2tog, yo, p2, 1/1 RC, p3, yo, ssk, k2tog, yo, k2, p1, k1.

Row 34: Rep Row 32.

Row 35: K1, p1, k6, p2, 1/1 RPC, 1/1 LPC, p1, k4, p1, 2/1 RPC, p1, 2/1 LPC, p1, k4, p1, 1/1 RPC, 1/1 LPC, p2, k6, p1, k1.

Row 36: Rep Row 30.

Row 37: K1, p1, k2, p5, 1/1 RPC, p2, 1/1 LPC, p4, 2/1 RPC, p3, 2/1 LPC, p4, 1/1 RPC, p2, 1/1 LPC, p5, k2, p1, k1.

Row 38: Rep Row 28.

Row 39: K1, p1, k2, p4, 1/1 RPC, p4, 1/1 LPC, p2, 2/1 RPC, p5, 2/1 LPC, p2, 1/1 RPC, p4, 1/1 LPC, p4, k2, p1, k1.

Row 40: Rep Row 26.

Row 41: K1, p1, k2, p3, 1/1 RPC, p1, k4, p1, 1/1 LPC, 2/1 RPC, p1, k1, yo, cdd, yo, k1, p1, 2/1 LPC, 1/1 RPC, p1, k4, p1, 1/1 LPC, p3, k2, p1, k1.

Row 42: Rep Row 22.

Row 43: K1, p1, k2, p3, k1, p2, yo, ssk, k2tog, yo, p2, 2/1 RC, p2, k1, yo, cdd, yo, k1, p2, 2/1 LC, p2, yo, ssk, k2tog, yo, p2, k1, p3, k2, p1, k1.

Row 44: Rep Row 22.

Row 45: K1, p1, k2, p3, 1/1 LPC, p1, k4, p1, 2/1 RPC, 1/1 LPC, p1, k1, yo, cdd, yo, k1, p1, 1/1 RPC, 2/1 LPC, p1, k4, p1, 1/1 RPC, p3, k2, p1, k1.

Row 46: Rep Row 20.

Row 47: K1, p1, k2, p4, 1/1 LPC, p4, 2/1 RPC, p2, 1/1 LPC, p5, 1/1 RPC, p2, 2/1 LPC, p4, 1/1 RPC, p4, k2, p1, k1.

Row 48: Rep Row 18.

Row 49: K1, p1, k2, p5, 1/1 LPC, p2, 2/1 RPC, p4, 1/1 RPC, p3, 1/1 RPC, p4, 2/1 LPC, p2, 1/1 RPC, p5, k2, p1, k1.

Row 50: Rep Row 16.

Row 51: K1, p1, k7, p1, 1/1 LPC, 2/1 RPC, p1, k4, p1, 1/1 LPC, p1, 1/1 RPC, p1, k4, p1, 2/1 LPC, 1/1 RPC, p1, k7, p1, k1.

Row 52: Rep Row 12.

Row 53: K1, p1, k3, yo, ssk, k2tog, yo, p2, 2/1 RC, p2, yo, ssk, k2tog, yo, p2, 1/1/1 RPC, p2, yo, ssk, k2tog, yo, p2, 2/1 LC, p2, yo, ssk, k2tog, yo, k3, p1, k1.

Row 54: Rep Row 12.

Row 55: K1, p1, k7, p1, 2/1 RPC, 1/1 LPC, p1, k4, p1, 1/1 RPC, p1, 1/1 LPC, p1, k4, p1, 1/1 RPC, 2/1 LPC, p1, k7, p1, k1.

Row 56: Rep Row 10.

Row 57: K1, p1, k2, p5, 2/1 RPC, p2, 1/1 LPC, p4, 1/1 RPC, p3, 1/1 LPC, p4, 1/1 RPC, p2, 2/1 LPC, p5, k2, p1, k1.

Row 58: Rep Row 8.

Row 59: K1, p1, k2, p4, 2/1 RPC, p4, 1/1 LPC, p2, 1/1 RPC, p2, k1, p2, 1/1 LPC, p2, 1/1 RPC, p4, 2/1 LPC, p4, k2, p1, k1.

Row 60: Rep Row 6.

Row 61: K1, p1, k2, p3, 2/1 RPC, p2, k2, p2, 1/1 LPC, 1/1 RPC, p2, k3, p2, 1/1 LPC, 1/1 RPC, p2, k2, p2, 2/1 LPC, p3, k2, p1, k1.

Row 62: Rep Row 4.

Row 63: Rep Row 3.

Row 64: Rep Row 2.

Row 65: Knit.

Bind (cast) off all sts knitwise.

Weave in ends and block to finished size.

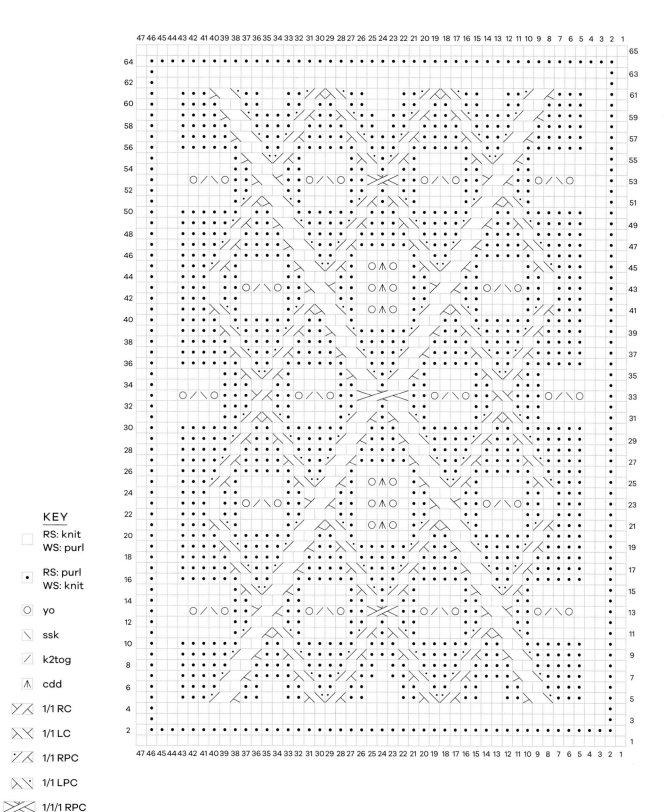

KEY

	RS: knit WS: purl
•	RS: purl WS: knit
O	yo
\	ssk
/	k2tog
∧	cdd
	1/1 RC
	1/1 LC
	1/1 RPC
	1/1 LPC
	1/1/1 RPC
	2/1 RC
	2/1 LC
	2/1 RPC
	2/1 LPC
	2/1/2 RPC

MOTTLED

DESIGNER: ANNA NIKIPIROWICZ

YARN

A - Grey (Izmir 073)

B - Green (Canberra 031)

NEEDLES

US size 4 (3.5mm) DPNs, or as needed to achieve gauge (tension)

ACCESSORIES

4 stitch markers, including one distinct for BOR

US size G-6 (4mm) crochet hook for provisional cast on

Waste yarn in contrasting colour

GAUGE (TENSION)

20 sts x 36 rounds = 4 x 4in (10 x 10cm) square

FINISHED SIZE

6 x 6in (15 x 15cm)

NOTES

This tile is worked in the round from the centre to the outer edge, starting with a crochet provisional cast on (see Techniques: Crochet Provisional Cast On).

When working the chart, the colour not in use should be stranded loosely across the back of the colour being used (see Techniques: Stranded Colourwork).

PATTERN

Using waste yarn and crochet hook, make 14 chains. Using yarn A and leaving a long tail, pick up and knit 12 sts in WS of crochet chain. Join to work in the round, being careful not to twist the sts. Mark the beginning of the round. 12 sts

Set-Up Round: [K3, yo, place marker] four times, with final marker for BOR.

Repeating chart four times in each round, work Rows 1 to 25 of chart, increasing before and after markers on rounds as indicated. 120 sts

Cut yarn B.

Bind (cast) off all sts.

Thread the yarn A cast-on yarn tail onto a tapestry needle. Unpick the provisional cast-on sts, placing them onto the tapestry needle. When all sts are released, pull tight to close the hole at the centre. Weave in ends and block to finished size.

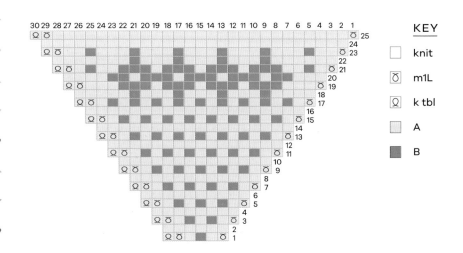

KEY

☐	knit
⊙	m1L
Ⓠ	k tbl
░	A
▓	B

HIDDEN TREASURE

DESIGNER: ARELLA SEATON

YARN

A - Cream (Lyon 078)

B - Dark Blue (Bucharest 001)

NEEDLES

US size 2.5 (3mm) needles, or as needed to achieve gauge (tension)

GAUGE (TENSION)

31 sts x 60 rows = 4 x 4in (10 x 10cm) square

FINISHED SIZE

6 x 6in (15 x 15cm)

KEY

☐ A

■ B

NOTES

Work this tile using mosaic knitting (see Techniques: Mosaic Knitting). Each chart row represents one RS row and one WS row. Knit sts that are the colour of the first st of the row, and slip the other colour.

PATTERN

Using yarn A, cast on 47 sts.

Work from chart as follows:

Row 1 (RS): Using yarn A, knit to end.

Row 1 (WS): Using yarn A, knit to end.

Row 2 (RS): Using yarn B, k1, slip 1 purlwise, k5, slip 1 purlwise, k1, [slip 1 purlwise, k13] twice, slip 1 purlwise, k1, slip 1 purlwise, k5, slip 1 purlwise, k1.

Row 2 (WS): Using yarn B, k1, move yarn to front, slip 1 purlwise, move yarn to back, k5, move yarn to front, slip 1 purlwise, move yarn to back, k1, [move yarn to front, slip 1 purlwise, move yarn to back, k13] twice, move yarn to front, slip 1 purlwise, move yarn to back, k1, move yarn to front, slip 1 purlwise, move yarn to back, k5, move yarn to front, slip 1 purlwise, move yarn to back, k1.

Continue working from chart until Row 45 WS has been completed.

Bind (cast) off all sts knitwise using yarn A.

Weave in ends and block to finished size.

BUTTONHOLES

DESIGNER: ASHLEY GIBBONS

YARN

Pink (Montreal 059)

NEEDLES

US size 2 (2.75mm) needles, or as needed to achieve gauge (tension)

GAUGE (TENSION)

30 sts x 40 rows = 4 x 4in (10 x 10cm) square

FINISHED SIZE

5¼ x 5¼in (13.5 x 13.5cm)

NOTES

This tile uses only knit and purl stitches to create a textured pattern. Slip the first stitch of each row purlwise.

PATTERN

Cast on 41 sts.

Row 1 (RS): Slip 1, k39, p1.

Row 2: Slip 1, *k3, p1, k1, p1; rep to last 4 sts, k3, p1.

Row 3: Slip 1, *p3, k3; rep to last 4 sts, p4.

Rows 4 to 7: Rep Rows 2 and 3 twice.

Row 8: Slip 1, *p1, k1, p1, k3; rep to last 4 sts, p1, k1, p2.

Row 9: Slip 1, *k3, p3; rep to last 4 sts, k3, p1.

Rows 10 to 13: Rep Rows 8 and 9 twice.

Rep Rows 2 to 13 four more times.

Bind (cast) off all sts knitwise.

Weave in ends and block to finished size.

WITH A TWIST

DESIGNER: JOANNE FOWLER

YARN

A - Cream (Lyon 078)

B - Lilac (Lima 055)

C - Light Blue (Ulsan 015)

D - Purple (Santiago 053)

E - Medium Blue (Kabul 004)

NEEDLES

US size 1.5 (2.5mm) needles, or as needed to achieve gauge (tension)

US size 1.5 (2.5mm) DPNs, or same size as gauge needles

GAUGE (TENSION)

21 sts x 42 rows = 4 x 4in (10 x 10cm) square

FINISHED SIZE

6 x 6in (15 x 15cm)

NOTES

This tile is worked in modular knitting, where multiple sections are worked by picking up stitches along previously completed sections. Each section is worked back and forth in rows of garter stitch. A central square is worked, then rounds of triangles are worked by picking up stitches and working short rows to shape. There is no need to wrap stitches for short rows, simply turn the work as instructed.

While it is helpful to weave in ends as you go, the ends should be woven in after completing the following round so that picking up stitches does not unravel previously woven in ends.

PATTERN

CENTRAL SQUARE

Using yarn A, cast on 8 sts.

Knit 14 rows in garter stitch.

Bind (cast) off knitwise.

ROUND 1 - SIDE 1

Row 1 (RS): Using yarn B, pick up a stitch in each of the bound-off (cast-off) sts of Central Square. 8 sts

Short Rows 2 and 3: K2, turn.

Short Rows 4 and 5: K4, turn.

Short Rows 6 and 7: K6, turn.

Row 8 (WS): Knit to end.

Bind (cast) off knitwise.

ROUND 1 - SIDE 2

Rotate Central Square to work on next side.

Row 1 (RS): Using yarn C, pick up a stitch in each garter ridge of Central Square. 8 sts

Rows 2 to 8: Work as for Side 1.

Bind (cast) off knitwise.

ROUND 1 - SIDE 3

Rotate Central Square and work as for Side 1 picking up in cast-on sts of Central Square using yarn B.

ROUND 1 - SIDE 4

Work as for Side 2.

ROUND 2 - SIDE 1

Row 1 (RS): Using yarn D, pick up 4 sts in the end of each garter ridge of a yarn C side plus 1 st in each bound-off (cast-off) st in the following yarn B side. 12 sts

Short Rows 2 and 3: K3, turn.

Short Rows 4 and 5: K6, turn.

Short Rows 6 and 7: K8, turn.

Row 8 (WS): Knit to end.

Bind (cast) off knitwise.

ROUND 2 - SIDES 2 TO 4

Rotate Central Square to work on next side, changing to yarn E for Sides 2 and 4 and yarn D for Side 3, repeating Rows 1 to 8.

ROUNDS 3 TO 6

Work in same way as for Round 2, alternating colours to work with yarns B and C on odd-numbered rounds and yarns D and E on even-numbered rounds, and picking up an additional 4 sts from bound-off (cast-off) edges in each subsequent round.

Round 3 picks up 16 total sts, and works short rows of 4, 8 and 12 sts. Round 4 picks up 20 total sts and works short rows of 5, 10 and 15 sts. Round 5 picks up 24 sts and works short rows of 6, 12 and 18 sts. Round 6 picks up 28 sts and works short rows of 7, 14 and 21 sts.

BORDER

Using yarn A and DPNs, starting in any corner, [pick up and knit 4 sts in the end of each garter ridge of a yarn C or D side plus a stitch in each of the bound-off (cast-off) sts in the following side] four times. Join to work in the round. 128 sts

Bind (cast) off as follows: *K2tog, slip st back to LH needle; rep from * to end.

Fasten off, pulling yarn through last st.

Weave in ends and block to finished size.

TRANSFORMATIVE

DESIGNER: ARELLA SEATON

YARN

A - Cream (Lyon 078)

B - Light Blue (Ulsan 015)

C - Dark Blue (Bucharest 001)

D - Black (Cairo 070)

NEEDLES

US size 2.5 (3mm) DPNs, or as needed to achieve gauge (tension)

ACCESSORIES

4 stitch markers, including one distinct for BOR

GAUGE (TENSION)

25 sts x 47 rounds = 4 x 4in (10 x 10cm) square

FINISHED SIZE

6½ x 6½in (16.5 x 16.5cm)

NOTES

This tile is worked in the round from the centre to the outer edge, with only one colour worked in each round. Slip all stitches purlwise with yarn stranded loosely across the back of the work.

SPECIAL ABBREVIATIONS

Rli: right lifted increase – lift the RH leg of st below next st on LH needle onto LH needle and knit it

Lli: left lifted increase – lift the LH leg of st 2 rows below st on RH needle onto LH needle and knit it through the back loop

PATTERN

Using yarn A, cast on 12 sts using a centre-out cast-on method (see Techniques: Centre-Out Cast On) or cast on with your preferred method, leaving a long yarn tail. Join to work in the round, being careful not to twist the sts. Mark the beginning of the round. 12 sts

Set-Up Round: [K3, place marker] four times, with final marker for BOR.

Repeating chart four times in each round, work Rows 1 to 46 of chart, increasing before and after markers on odd-numbered rounds as indicated and joining in yarns as required. 196 sts

Cut all yarns except yarn A.

Bind (cast) off all sts.

Use the cast-on yarn tail to close the hole at the centre if needed.

Weave in ends and block to finished size.

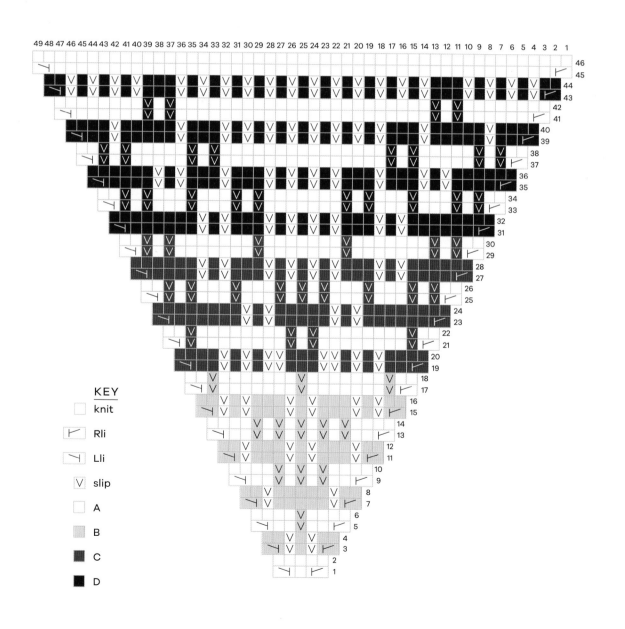

KEY

☐	knit
⌐	Rli
¬	Lli
V	slip
☐	A
☐	B
■	C
■	D

ROMAN URNS

DESIGNER: LILY LANGMAN

YARN

A – Cream (Lyon 078)

B – Blue (Washington 013)

C – Yellow (Brasov 038)

D – Dark Green (Karachi 016)

NEEDLES

US size 1.5 (2.5mm) needles, or as needed to achieve gauge (tension)

GAUGE (TENSION)

29 sts x 45 rows = 4 x 4in (10 x 10cm) square

FINISHED SIZE

7¼ x 5½in (18 x 14cm)

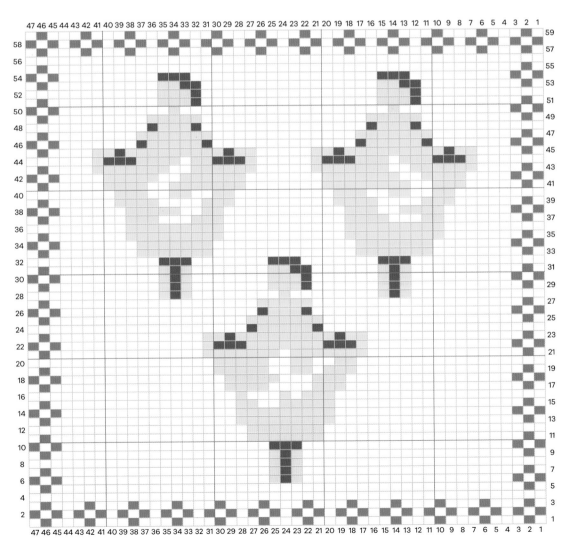

KEY

- ☐ RS: knit WS: purl
- ☐ A
- ☐ B
- ☐ C
- ☐ D

NOTES

This tile is knitted with a border of garter stitch on the top and bottom edges and 3 garter stitches on each side. The chart is worked in stockinette (stocking) stitch.

When working with two or three colours at once, the colours not in use should be stranded loosely across the back of the colour being used (see Techniques: Stranded Colourwork).

When stranding the yarn becomes difficult, use a separate ball of yarn for each colour and twist the yarn about to be used around the colour just used to link yarns together on WS to avoid a hole (see Techniques: Intarsia).

If you prefer to work a smaller tile without the border, cast on 47 stitches using yarn A, work the chart, then bind (cast) off using yarn A.

PATTERN

Using yarn A, cast on 53 sts.

Work 4 rows of garter stitch.

Join in other colours as needed and work as follows:

Row 1 (RS): K3 using yarn A, knit Row 1 of chart, k3 using yarn A.

Row 2: K3 using A, purl Row 2 of chart, k3 using yarn A.

Keeping first 3 sts and last 3 sts in garter stitch using yarn A throughout, continue until chart is complete.

Cut all colours except yarn A.

Work 3 rows of garter stitch.

Bind (cast) off all sts.

Weave in ends and block to finished size.

WHIMSICAL WONDER

DESIGNER: ASHLEIGH WEMPE

YARN

A - Medium Orange (Sevilla 076)

B - Dark Orange (Mexico City 075)

C - Light Grey (Cota 024)

D - Dark Blue (Bucharest 001)

NEEDLES

US size 8 (5mm) DPNs

US size 7 (4.5mm) DPNs, or as needed to achieve gauge (tension)

ACCESSORIES

4 stitch markers, including one distinct for BOR

GAUGE (TENSION)

15 sts x 27 rounds = 4 x 4in (10 x 10cm) square using yarn held double on US size 7 (4.5mm) needles

FINISHED SIZE

7 x 7in (18 x 18cm)

NOTES

This tile is worked in the round from the outer edge to the centre. The yarn is held double throughout. Use two separate balls or find both ends of the ball. There is no border and the stockinette (stocking) stitch fabric will tend to roll even after blocking, so this design is intended to be part of a larger project.

When working the chart, the colour not in use should be stranded loosely across the back of the colour being used (see Techniques: Stranded Colourwork).

PATTERN

Using US size 8 (5mm) DPNs, and with one strand of yarn A and one strand of yarn B held together, cast on 108 sts. Join to work in the round, being careful not to twist the sts.

Cut yarns A and B.

Change to US size 7 (4.5mm) DPNs.

Using two strands of yarn C as MC and two strands of yarn D as CC, work as follows:

Round 1: [Work Row 1 of chart, place marker] four times, with final marker for BOR.

Continue working as set, slipping markers and working decreases as shown, until chart is complete. 12 sts

Cut all yarn strands and thread MC tail through remaining sts, pulling tight to close the hole.

Weave in ends and block to finished size.

HORIZON

DESIGNER: ANNI HOWARD

YARN

A - Orange (Quebec 077)

B - Blue (Lahore 014)

C - Cream (Lyon 078)

NEEDLES

US size 3 (3.25mm) needles, or as needed to achieve gauge (tension)

GAUGE (TENSION)

34 sts x 64 rows = 4 x 4in (10 x 10cm) square

FINISHED SIZE

6 x 6in (15 x 15cm)

NOTES

Work this tile using mosaic knitting (see Techniques: Mosaic Knitting). Each chart row represents one RS row and one WS row. Knit stitches that are the colour of the first stitch of the row, and slip the other colour.

KEY

☐ knit

◩ k2tog

◪ ssk

☐ MC

■ CC

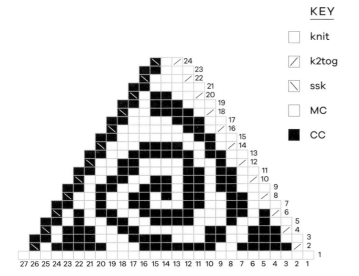

PATTERN

Using yarn A, cast on 51 sts.

Work from chart as follows:

Row 1 (RS): Using yarn A, knit to end.

Row 1 (WS): Using yarn A, knit to end.

Row 2 (RS): Using yarn B, k1, *slip 1 purlwise, k1; rep from * to end.

Row 2 (WS): Using yarn B, k1, *move yarn to front, slip 1 purlwise, move yarn to back, k1; rep from * to end.

Continue working from chart until Row 48 WS has been completed, cutting yarn A and joining yarn C after Row 26.

Bind (cast) off all sts knitwise using yarn B.

Weave in ends and block to finished size.

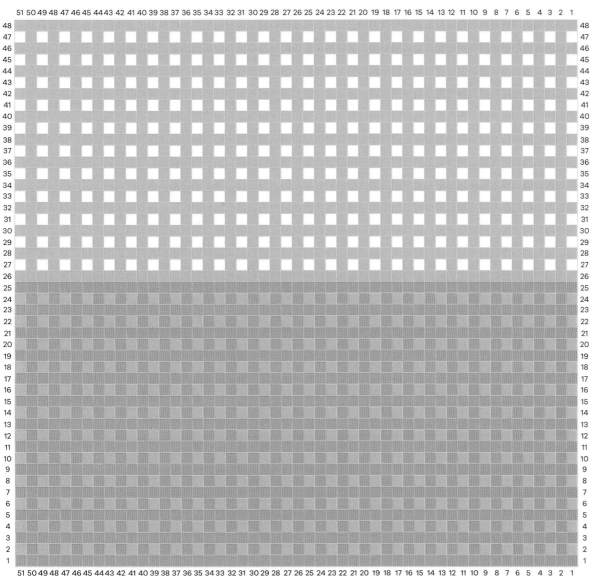

KEY

- A
- B
- C

ATTICA

DESIGNER: ANNAPLEXIS

YARN

A - Wine Red (Rabat 041)

B - Pale Yellow (Delhi 039)

NEEDLES

US size 1.5 (2.5mm) DPNs, or as needed to achieve gauge (tension)

ACCESSORIES

4 stitch markers, including one distinct for BOR

GAUGE (TENSION)

29 sts x 45 rounds = 4 x 4in (10 x 10cm) square

FINISHED SIZE

6¼ x 6¼in (16 x 16cm)

NOTES

This tile is worked in the round from the outer edge to the centre, working from the chart and including a garter stitch border.

When working the chart, the colour not in use should be stranded loosely across the back of the colour being used (see Techniques: Stranded Colourwork).

PATTERN

Using yarn A, cast on 180 sts. Join to work in the round, being careful not to twist the sts.

Round 1: [Work Row 1 of chart, place marker] four times, with final marker for BOR.

Continue working as set, slipping markers and working decreases as shown, and joining in yarn B as needed, until chart is complete. 12 sts

Cut both yarn strands and thread tail of yarn B through remaining sts, pulling tight to close the hole.

Weave in ends and block to finished size.

KEY

☐ knit

• purl

╱ k2tog

╲ ssk

■ A

☐ B

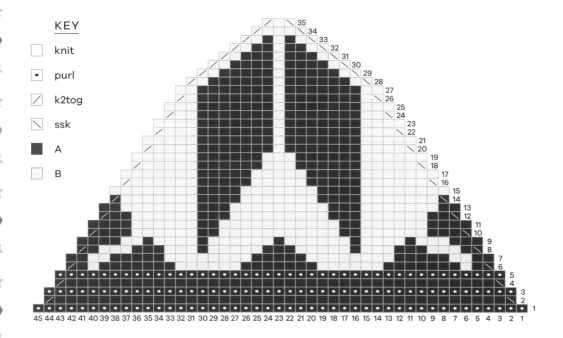

CABLED OVER

DESIGNER: JOANNE FOWLER

YARN

Cream (Toulouse 030)

NEEDLES

US size 1.5 (2.5mm) needles, or as needed to achieve gauge (tension)

ACCESSORIES

Cable needle

GAUGE (TENSION)

43 sts x 43 rows = 4 x 4in (10 x 10cm) measured over pattern when rib side section is not stretched out

FINISHED SIZE

6 x 6in (15 x 15cm)

SPECIAL ABBREVIATIONS

Rli: right lifted increase – lift the RH leg of st below next st on LH needle onto LH needle and knit it

Lli: left lifted increase – lift the LH leg of st 2 rows below st on RH needle onto LH needle and knit it through the back loop

3/2 LPC: 3 over 2 left purl cross – slip 3 sts to cable needle, hold at front of work, p2 from LH needle, k3 from cable needle

3/2 RPC: 3 over 2 right purl cross – slip 2 sts to cable needle, hold at back of work, k3 from LH needle, p2 from cable needle

3/3 LPC: 3 over 3 left purl cross – slip 3 sts to cable needle, hold at front of work, p3 from LH needle, k3 from cable needle

3/3 RPC: 3 over 3 right purl cross – slip 3 sts to cable needle, hold at back of work, k3 from LH needle, p3 from cable needle

3/3 RC: 3 over 3 right cross – slip 3 sts to cable needle, hold at back of work, k3 from LH needle, k3 from cable needle

3/3 LC: 3 over 3 left cross – slip 3 sts to cable needle, hold at front of work, k3 from LH needle, k3 from cable needle

NOTES

The tile is knitted diagonally from one corner to another with the right side featuring stockinette (stocking) stitch cables on a reverse stockinette (stocking) stitch background. When multiple Cabled Over tiles are seamed together, various eye-catching patterns can form depending on the arrangement.

If you find it fiddly to work the lifted increases in Row 1 as you are lifting from the cast-on row, you can substitute a twisted yarn over or backwards loop (e-loop) increase on this row instead, as long as it does not leave a hole.

The cables are worked with knit and purl stitches (see Special Abbreviations).

During blocking and seaming, take care not to stretch out the rib sections.

Rows 1 to 91 are also shown in the chart. Note that after the cast on, Row 1 is a WS row.

PATTERN

Using long tail cast-on method (see Techniques: Long Tail/Continental Cast On), cast on 2 sts.

INCREASE SECTION

Row 1 (WS): Rli, p2, Lli. 4 sts

Row 2: Rli, k4, Lli. 6 sts

Row 3: Rli, p6, Lli. 8 sts

Row 4: Rli, p1, 3/3 LC, p1, Lli. 10 sts

Row 5: Rli, k2, p6, k2, Lli. 12 sts

Row 6: Rli, p3, k6, p3, Lli. 14 sts

Row 7: Rli, p1, k3, p6, k3, p1, Lli. 16 sts

Row 8: Rli, k2, p3, k6, p3, k2, Lli. 18 sts

Row 9: Rli, p3, k3, p6, k3, p3, Lli. 20 sts

Row 10: Rli, p1, k3, p3, k6, p3, k3, p1, Lli. 22 sts

Row 11: Rli, k2, p3, k3, p6, k3, p3, k2, Lli. 24 sts

Row 12: Rli, p3, 3/3 LPC, 3/3 LC, 3/3 RPC, p3, Lli. 26 sts

Row 13: Rli, k7, p12, k7, Lli. 28 sts

Row 14: Rli, p8, k12, p8, Lli. 30 sts

Row 15: Rli, k9, p12, k9, Lli. 32 sts

Row 16: Rli, p10, [3/3 RC] twice, p10, Lli. 34 sts

Row 17: Rli, k11, p12, k11, Lli. 36 sts

Row 18: Rli, p12, k12, p12, Lli. 38 sts

Row 19: Rli, k13, p12, k13, Lli. 40 sts

Row 20: Rli, p14, k3, 3/3 LC, k3, p14, Lli. 42 sts

Row 21: Rli, k15, p12, k15, Lli. 44 sts

Row 22: Rli, p16, k12, p16, Lli. 46 sts

Row 23: Rli, k17, p12, k17, Lli. 48 sts

Row 24: Rli, p18, [3/3 RC] twice, p18, Lli. 50 sts

BEGIN RIB SECTION AT SIDES AND CONTINUE INCREASING

Row 25: Rli, p1, k18, p12, k18, p1, Lli. 52 sts

Row 26: Rli, k2, p18, k12, p18, k2, Lli. 54 sts

Row 27: Rli, p3, k18, p12, k18, p3, Lli. 56 sts

Row 28: Rli, p1, k3, p15, 3/3 RPC, 3/3 LC, 3/3 LPC, p15, k3, p1, Lli. 58 sts

Row 29: Rli, k2, p3, k15, p3, k3, p6, k3, p3, k15, p3, k2, Lli. 60 sts

Row 30: Rli, p3, k3, p15, k3, p3, k6, p3, k3, p15, k3, p3, Lli. 62 sts

Row 31: Rli, p1, k3, p3, k15, p3, k3, p6, k3, p3, k15, p3, k3, p1, Lli. 64 sts

Row 32: Rli, k2, p3, k3, p12, 3/3 RPC, p3, k6, p3, 3/3 LPC, p12, k3, p3, k2, Lli. 66 sts

Row 33: Rli, p3, k3, p3, k12, p3, k6, p6, k6, p3, k12, p3, k3, p3, Lli. 68 sts

Row 34: Rli, p1, k3, p3, k3, p12, k3, p6, k6, p6, k3, p12, k3, p3, k3, p1, Lli. 70 sts

Row 35: Rli, k2, p3, k3, p3, k12, p3, k6, p6, k6, p3, k12, p3, k3, p3, k2, Lli. 72 sts

Row 36: Rli, [p3, k3] twice, p9, 3/3 RC, [p6, 3/3 LC] twice, p9, [k3, p3] twice, Lli. 74 sts

Row 37: Rli, p1, [k3, p3] twice, k9, [p6, k6] twice, p6, k9, [p3, k3] twice, p1, Lli. 76 sts

Row 38: Rli, k2, [p3, k3] twice, p9, [k6, p6] twice, k6, p9, [k3, p3] twice, k1, Lli. 78 sts

Row 39: Rli, p3, [k3, p3] twice, k9, [p6, k6] twice, p6, k9, [p3, k3] twice, p3, Lli. 80 sts

Row 40: Rli, p1, k3, [p3, k3] twice, p9, [k6, p6] twice, k6, p9, [k3, p3] twice, k3, p1, Lli. 82 sts

Row 41: Rli, k2, p3, [k3, p3] twice, k9, [p6, k6] twice, p6, k9, [p3, k3] twice, p3, k2, Lli. 84 sts

Row 42: Rli, [p3, k3] three times, p9, [k6, p6] twice, k6, p9, [k3, p3] three times, Lli. 86 sts

Row 43: Rli, p1, [k3, p3] three times, k9, [p6, k6] twice, p6, k9, [p3, k3] three times, p1, Lli. 88 sts

Row 44: Rli, k2, [p3, k3] three times, p9, 3/3 RC, [p6, 3/3 LC] twice, p9, [k3, p3] three times, k2, Lli. 90 sts

Row 45: Rli, p3, [k3, p3] three times, k9, [p6, k6] twice, p6, k9, [p3, k3] three times, p3, Lli. 92 sts

BEGIN DECREASE SECTION

Row 46: Skpo, k2, [p3, k3] three times, p9, [k6, p6] twice, k6, p9, [k3, p3] three times, k2, k2tog. 90 sts

Row 47: P2tog, p1, [k3, p3] three times, k9, [p6, k6] twice, p6, k9, [p3, k3] three times, p1, p2tog. 88 sts

Row 48: Skpo, [p3, k3] three times, p6, 3/3 RPC, 3/3 LPC, p3, k6, p3, 3/3 RPC, 3/3 LPC, p6, [k3, p3] three times, k2tog. 86 sts

Row 49: P2tog, k2, p3, [k3, p3] twice, k6, p3, k6, p3, k3, p6, k3, p3, k6, p3, k6, [p3, k3] twice, p3, k2, p2tog. 84 sts

Row 50: Skpo, p1, k3, [p3, k3] twice, [p6, k3] twice, p3, k6, p3, [k3, p6] twice, [k3, p3] twice, k3, p1, k2tog. 82 sts

Row 51: P2tog, p3, [k3, p3] twice, [k6, p3] twice, k3, p6, k3, [p3, k6] twice, [p3, k3] twice, p3, p2tog. 80 sts

Row 52: Skpo, k2, [p3, k3] twice, p3, 3/3 RPC, p6, 3/3 LPC, 3/3 LC, 3/3 RPC, p6, 3/3 LPC, p3, [k3, p3] twice, k2, k2tog. 78 sts

Row 53: P2tog, p1, [k3, p3] three times, k12, p12, k12, [p3, k3] three times, p1, p2tog. 76 sts

Row 54: Skpo, [p3, k3] three times, p12, k12, p12, [k3, p3] three times, k2tog. 74 sts

Row 55: P2tog, k2, p3, [k3, p3] twice, k12, p12, k12, [p3, k3] twice, p3, k2, p2tog. 72 sts

Row 56: Skpo, p1, k3, [p3, k3] twice, p12, [3/3 RC] twice, p12, [k3, p3] twice, k3, p1, k2tog. 70 sts

Row 57: P2tog, p3, [k3, p3] twice, k12, p12, k12, [p3, k3] twice, p3, p2tog. 68 sts

Row 58: Skpo, k2, [p3, k3] twice, p12, k12, p12, [k3, p3] twice, k2, k2tog. 66 sts

Row 59: P2tog, p1, [k3, p3] twice, k12, p12, k12, [p3, k3] twice, p1, p2tog. 64 sts

Row 60: Skpo, [p3, k3] twice, p12, k3, 3/3 LC, k3, p12, [k3, p3] twice, k2tog. 62 sts

Row 61: P2tog, k2, p3, k3, p3, k12, p12, k12, p3, k3, p3, k2, p2tog. 60 sts

Row 62: Skpo, p1, k3, p3, k3, p12, k12, p12, k3, p3, k3, p1, k2tog. 58 sts

Row 63: P2tog, p3, k3, p3, k12, p12, k12, p3, k3, p3, p2tog. 56 sts

Row 64: Skpo, k2, p3, k3, p12, [3/3 RC] twice, p12, k3, p3, k2, k2tog. 54 sts

Row 65: P2tog, p1, k3, p3, k12, p12, k12, p3, k3, p1, p2tog. 52 sts

Row 66: Skpo, p3, k3, p12, k12, p12, k3, p3, k2tog. 50 sts

Row 67: P2tog, k2, p3, k12, p12, k12, p3, k2, p2tog. 48 sts

Row 68: Skpo, p1, k3, p9, 3/3 RPC, 3/3 LC, 3/3 LPC, p9, k3, p1, k2tog. 46 sts

Row 69: P2tog, p3, k9, p3, k3, p6, k3, p3, k9, p3, p2tog. 44 sts

Row 70: Skpo, k2, p9, k3, p3, k6, p3, k3, p9, k2, k2tog. 42 sts

Row 71: P2tog, p1, k9, p3, k3, p6, k3, p3, k9, p1, p2tog. 40 sts

END RIB SECTION AT SIDES AND CONTINUE DECREASING

Row 72: Skpo, p6, 3/3 RPC, p3, k6, p3, 3/3 LPC, p6, k2tog. 38 sts

Row 73: P2tog, k5, p3, k6, p6, k6, p3, k5, p2tog. 36 sts

Row 74: Skpo, p4, k3, p6, k6, p6, k3, p4, k2tog. 34 sts

Row 75: P2tog, k3, p3, k6, p6, k6, p3, k3, p2tog. 32 sts

Row 76: Skpo, 3/2 RPC, p6, 3/3 LC, p6, 3/2 LPC, k2tog. 30 sts

Row 77: P2tog, p2, k8, p6, k8, p2, p2tog. 28 sts

Row 78: Skpo, k1, p8, k6, p8, k1, k2tog. 26 sts

Row 79: P2tog, k8, p6, k8, p2tog. 24 sts

Row 80: Skpo, p7, k6, p7, k2tog. 22 sts

Row 81: P2tog, k6, p6, k6, p2tog. 20 sts

Row 82: Skpo, p5, k6, p5, k2tog. 18 sts

Row 83: P2tog, k4, p6, k4, p2tog. 16 sts

Row 84: Skpo, p3, 3/3 LC, p3, k2tog. 14 sts

Row 85: P2tog, k2, p6, k2, p2tog. 12 sts

Row 86: Skpo, p1, k6, p1, k2tog. 10 sts

Row 87: P2tog, p6, p2tog. 8 sts

Row 88: Skpo, k4, k2tog. 6 sts

Row 89: P2tog, p2, p2tog. 4 sts

Row 90: Skpo, k2tog. 2 sts

Row 91: P2tog. 1 st

Fasten off, pulling yarn through last st.

Weave in ends and block to finished size, taking care not to stretch out the ribbed sections.

KEY

⏝	cast on		3/2 LPC
☐	RS: knit WS: purl		3/2 RPC
•	RS: purl WS: knit		3/3 RC
⌐	RS: Rli WS: Lli		3/3 LC
⌐	RS: Lli WS: Rli		3/3 RPC
◸	RS: skpo WS: p2tog		3/3 LPC
◹	RS: k2tog WS: p2tog		

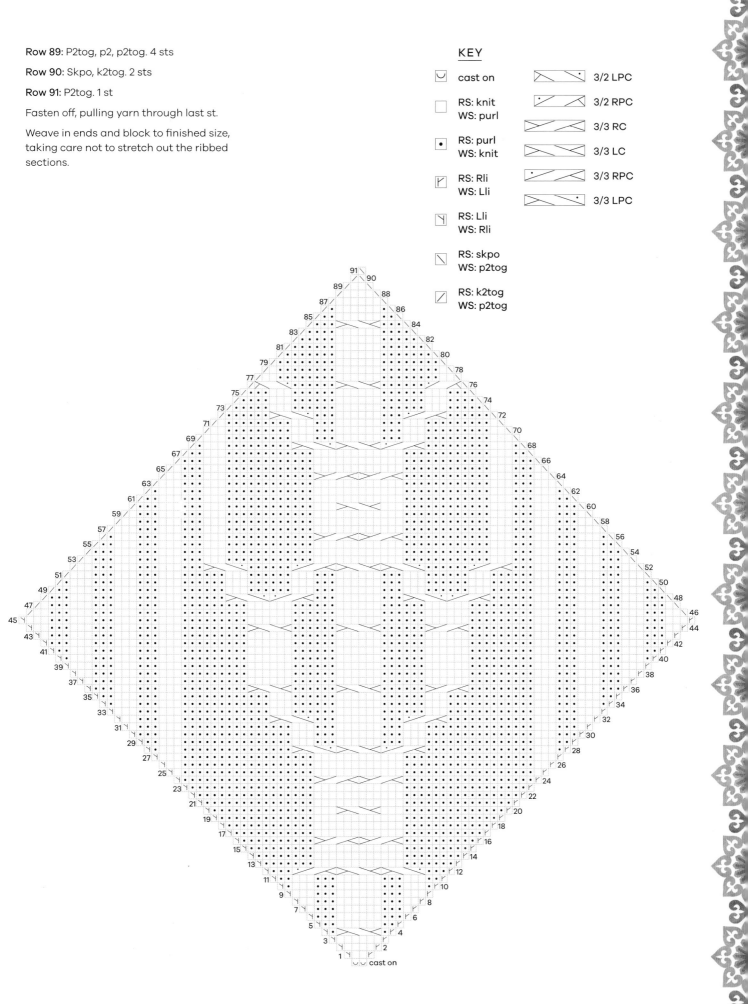

cast on

HONEYCOMB

DESIGNER: DANIELLE HOLKE

YARN

A - Rust (Kraków 064)

B - Light Teal (Marseille 019)

NEEDLES

US size 2 (2.75mm) needles, or as needed to achieve gauge (tension)

GAUGE (TENSION)

36 sts x 46 rows = 4 x 4in (10 x 10cm) square

FINISHED SIZE

6¼ x 6¼in (16 x 16cm)

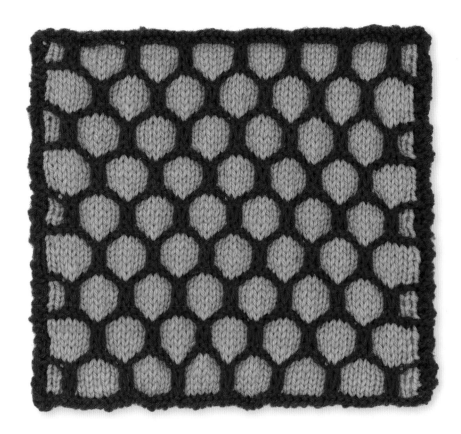

KEY

☐	RS: knit WS: purl
⊡	WS: knit
ⱽ	slip 1 knitwise
⋁	slip 1 purlwise
■	A
☐	B

NOTES

Slipped stitches create a textured hexagon pattern that seems to 'float' over the stockinette (stocking) stitch background. The tile is worked with a border in garter stitch, with stitches slipped at the start of rows to create a firm edge. Work slip stitches at the start of rows knitwise, holding the yarn in back.

For the pattern repeat, slip stitches purlwise, stranding the yarn along the WS of the work. When working a RS row hold the yarn at the back of the work, and when working a WS row hold the yarn at the front. Make sure not to pull too tightly so that the fabric does not pucker.

Rows 3 to 18 are also shown in the chart.

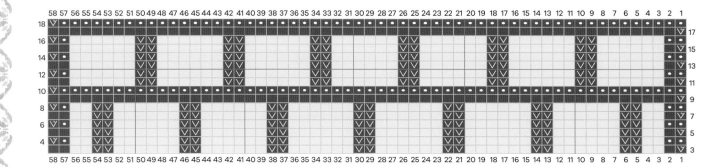

PATTERN

Using yarn A, cast on 58 sts.

Row 1 (RS): Knit.

Row 2: Slip 1 knitwise, knit to end.

Join in yarn B.

Row 3: Slip 1 knitwise, k1 using yarn A, k2 using yarn B, *slip 2 purlwise, k6 using yarn B; rep from * to last 6 sts, slip 2 purlwise, k2 using yarn B, k2 using yarn A.

Row 4: Slip 1 knitwise, k1 using yarn A, p2 using yarn B, *slip 2 purlwise, p6 using yarn B; rep from * to last 6 sts, slip 2 purlwise, p2 using yarn B, k3 using yarn A.

Rows 5 to 8: Rep Rows 3 and 4 twice.

Rows 9 and 10: Using yarn A, slip 1 knitwise, knit to end.

Row 11: Slip 1 knitwise, k1 using yarn A, k6 using yarn B, *slip 2 purlwise, k6 using yarn B; rep from * to last 2 sts, k2 using yarn A.

Row 12: Slip 1 knitwise, k1 using yarn A, p6 using yarn B, *slip 2 purlwise, p6 using yarn B; rep from * to last 2 sts, k2 using yarn A.

Rows 13 to 16: Rep Rows 11 and 12 twice.

Rows 17 and 18: Using yarn A, slip 1 knitwise, knit to end.

Rows 19 to 66: Rep Rows 3 to 18 three times.

Rows 67 to 72: Rep Rows 3 to 8.

Cut yarn B.

Rows 73 and 74: Using yarn A, slip 1 knitwise, knit to end.

Bind (cast) off all sts using yarn A.

Weave in ends and block to finished size.

PINK CANNA

DESIGNER: ANNA NIKIPIROWICZ

YARN

Pink (Montreal 059)

NEEDLES

US size 4 (3.5mm) DPNs, or as needed to achieve gauge (tension)

ACCESSORIES

Stitch marker

US size G-6 (4mm) crochet hook for provisional cast on

Waste yarn in contrasting colour

GAUGE (TENSION)

18 sts x 34 rounds = 4 x 4in (10 x 10cm) square

FINISHED SIZE

6¼ x 6¼in (16 x 15cm)

NOTES

This tile is worked in the round from the centre to the outer edge, starting with a crochet provisional cast on (see Techniques: Crochet Provisional Cast On).

When working into a double yarn over in the next round (yo2), work as [p1, k1 tbl].

PATTERN

Using waste yarn and crochet hook, make 10 chains. Using working yarn and leaving a long tail, pick up and knit 8 sts in WS of crochet chain. Join to work in the round, being careful not to twist the sts. Mark the beginning of the round. 8 sts

Round 1: [K2, yo] four times. 12 sts

Round 2 and even-numbered rounds to Round 24: Knit to end, working [p1, k1 tbl] into any yo2 from previous round.

Round 3: [Yo, k2, yo, k1 tbl] four times. 20 sts

Round 5: [Yo, k4, yo, k1 tbl] four times. 28 sts

Round 7: [Yo, k6, yo, k1 tbl] four times. 36 sts

Round 9: [Yo, k8, yo, k1 tbl] four times. 44 sts

Round 11: [Yo, k10, yo, k1 tbl] four times. 52 sts

Round 13: [Yo, k12, yo, k1 tbl] four times. 60 sts

Round 15: [Yo2, ssk, k10, k2tog, yo2, k1 tbl] four times. 68 sts

Round 17: [Yo, k2, yo, ssk, k8, k2tog, yo, k2, yo, k1 tbl] four times. 76 sts

Round 19: [Yo, k1, k2tog, yo, k1, yo, ssk, k6, k2tog, yo, k1, yo, ssk, k1, yo, k1 tbl] four times. 84 sts

Round 21: [Yo2, sl 1, k2tog, psso, yo, k1, k2tog, yo2, ssk, k4, k2tog, yo2, ssk, k1, yo, sl 1, k2tog, psso, yo2, k1 tbl] four times. 92 sts

Round 23: [Yo, k2, yo, ssk, k2tog, yo, k2, yo, ssk, k2, k2tog, yo, k2, yo, ssk, k2tog, yo, k2, yo, k1 tbl] four times. 100 sts

Round 25: [Yo, k1, k2tog, yo2, sl 1, k2tog, psso, yo, k1, k2tog, yo, k1, yo, ssk, k2tog, yo, k1, yo, ssk, k1, yo, sl 1, k2tog, psso, yo2, ssk, k1, yo, k1 tbl] four times. 108 sts

Round 26: Knit to end, working [p1, k1 tbl] into any yo2.

Bind (cast) off all sts.

Thread cast-on yarn tail onto a tapestry needle. Unpick the provisional cast-on sts, placing them onto the tapestry needle. When all sts are released, pull tight to close the hole at the centre. Weave in ends and block to finished size.

UNFOLDING

DESIGNER: SYLVIA WATTS-CHERRY

YARN

A - Pink (Montreal 059)

B - Yellow (Istanbul 037)

C - Blue (Washington 013)

NEEDLES

US size 1.5 (2.5mm) needles, or as needed to achieve gauge (tension)

GAUGE (TENSION)

28 sts x 56 rows = 4 x 4in (10 x 10cm) square

FINISHED SIZE

6 x 6in (15 x 15cm)

NOTES

This tile is worked in garter stitch using intarsia (see Techniques: Intarsia), with each block of colour knit from a separate ball or bobbin of yarn. Twist the yarn about to be used around the colour just used to link yarns together on WS to avoid a hole.

PATTERN

Using cable cast-on method (see Techniques: Cable Cast On) and yarn A, cast on 42 sts.

Work Rows 1 to 84 of chart, joining in and changing colours as indicated.

Bind (cast) off all sts knitwise using yarn A.

Weave in ends, closing any gaps with yarn tails at colour changes, and block to finished size.

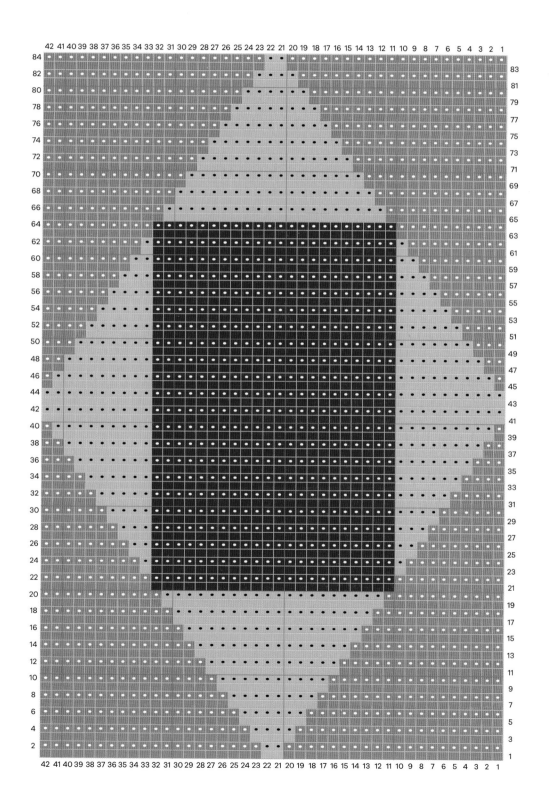

KEY

☐ RS: knit

⊡ WS: knit

▨ A

▨ B

■ C

CIRCUIT BOARD

DESIGNER: CARMEN JORISSEN

YARN

A - Lavender (Johannesburg 054)

B - Beige (Buenos Aires 067)

NEEDLES

US size 2.5 (3mm) needles, or as needed to achieve gauge (tension)

GAUGE (TENSION)

31 sts x 30 rows = 4 x 4in (10 x 10cm) square

FINISHED SIZE

5¾ x 5¾in (14.5 x 14.5cm)

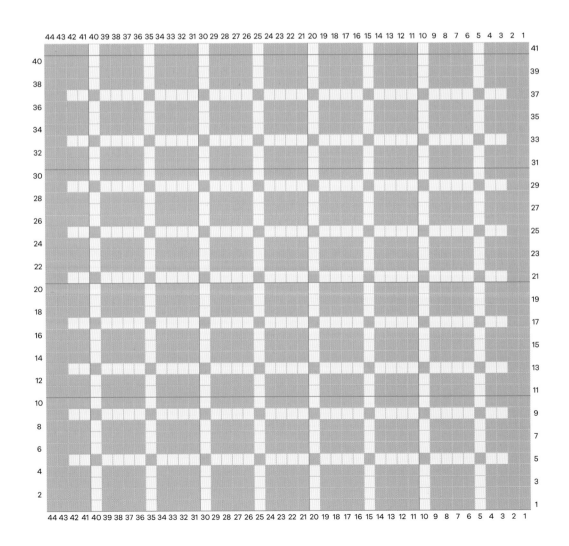

KEY

☐ RS: knit
WS: purl

▨ A

☐ B

NOTES

This tile is worked in stockinette (stocking) stitch following the colourwork chart. The colour not in use should be stranded loosely across the back of the colour being used (see Techniques: Stranded Colourwork).

To make your colourwork look neat, wrap yarn B at the start of every row, preferably on the second stitch, as follows:

On RS rows, insert RH needle into next stitch (to be worked in yarn A), lay yarn B horizontally from right to left over RH needle, knit the stitch using yarn A. Yarn B is now wrapped. Make sure yarn B is not being pulled through the stitch.

On WS rows, insert RH needle into next stitch (to be worked in yarn A), hold yarn B up so that it lays vertically across RH needle, purl the stitch using yarn A.

PATTERN

Using yarn A, cast on 44 sts.

Set-Up Row (WS): Using yarn A, purl to end.

Join in yarn B.

Work Rows 1 to 41 of chart.

Cut yarn B.

Next Row (WS): Using yarn A, purl to end.

Bind (cast) off all sts.

Weave in ends and block to finished size.

DIAMOND SIEVE

DESIGNER: ANNIKEN ALLIS

YARN

Indigo Blue (Dallas 003)

NEEDLES

US size 4 (3.5mm) needles, or as needed to achieve gauge (tension)

GAUGE (TENSION)

24 sts x 37 rows = 4 x 4in (10 x 10cm) square

FINISHED SIZE

5½ x 6in (14 x 15cm)

NOTES

This tile is worked in a garter stitch lace pattern. In the row after a double yarn over (yo2), work the second stitch of the double yarn over through the back loop.

Rows 1 to 20 are also shown in the chart.

PATTERN

Cast on 34 sts.

Work 3 rows of garter stitch.

Row 1 (RS): K3, *k1 tbl, k4, k2tog, yo2, ssk, k5; rep from * to last 3 sts, k3.

Row 2 (WS): K3, *k7, k1 tbl, k6; rep from * to last 3 sts, k3.

Row 3: K3, *k3, [k2tog, yo2, ssk] twice, k3; rep from * to last 3 sts, k3.

Row 4: K3, *k5, k1 tbl, k3, k1 tbl, k4; rep from * to last 3 sts, k3.

Row 5: K3, *k1, [k2tog, yo2, ssk] three times, k1; rep from * to last 3 sts, k3.

Row 6: K3, *[k3, k1 tbl] three times, k2; rep from * to last 3 sts, k3.

Row 7: K3, *k3, [k2tog, yo2, ssk] twice, k1 tbl, k2; rep from * to last 3 sts, k3.

Row 8: K3, *k5, k1 tbl, k3, k1 tbl, k4; rep from * to last 3 sts, k3.

Row 9: K3, *k5, k2tog, yo2, ssk, k1 tbl, k4; rep from * to last 3 sts, k3.

Row 10: K3, *k7, k1 tbl, k6; rep from * to last 3 sts, k3.

Row 11: K3, *yo, ssk, k5, k1 tbl, k4, k2tog, yo; rep from * to last 3 sts, k3.

Row 12: K3, *k1 tbl, k13; rep from * to last 3 sts, k3.

Row 13: K3, *k2tog, yo2, ssk, k6, k2tog, yo2, ssk; rep from * to last 3 sts, k3.

Row 14: K3, *k2, k1 tbl, k9, k1 tbl, k1; rep from * to last 3 sts, k3.

Row 15: K3, *yo, ssk, k2tog, yo2, ssk, k2, k2tog, yo2, ssk, k2tog, yo; rep from * to last 3 sts, k3.

Row 16: K3, *k1 tbl, k3, k1 tbl, k5, k1 tbl, k3; rep from * to last 3 sts, k3.

Row 17: K3, *k2tog, yo2, ssk, k1 tbl, k5, k2tog, yo2, ssk; rep from * to last 3 sts, k3.

Row 18: K3, *k2, k1 tbl, k9, k1 tbl, k1; rep from * to last 3 sts, k3.

Row 19: K3, *yo, ssk, k1 tbl, k9, k2tog, yo; rep from * to last 3 sts, k3.

Row 20: K3, *k1 tbl, k13; rep from * to last 3 sts, k3.

Rep Rows 1 to 20, then rep Rows 1 to 10 only once again.

Work 3 rows of garter stitch.

Bind (cast) off all sts knitwise.

Weave in ends and block to finished size.

VICTORIAN FLOWER

· · · · · · · · · · · · · · · · · ·

DESIGNER: HELEN BIRCH

YARN

A - Cream (Lyon 078)

B - Orange (Tripoli 074)

C - Blue (Boston 011)

D - Red (Naples 043)

NEEDLES

US size 2.5 (3mm) needles, or as needed to achieve gauge (tension)

GAUGE (TENSION)

29 sts x 40 rows = 4 x 4in (10 x 10cm) square

FINISHED SIZE

6¼ x 6½in (16 x 16.5cm)

NOTES

This design works the seed (moss) stitch border as part of the motif.

When working with two or three colours at once, the colours not in use should be stranded loosely across the back of the colour being used (see Techniques: Stranded Colourwork).

When stranding the yarn becomes difficult, use a separate ball of yarn for each colour and twist the yarn about to be used around the colour just used to link yarns together on WS to avoid a hole (see Techniques: Intarsia).

KEY

☐ RS: knit

• WS: knit

╱ k2tog

○ yo

╲ ssk

Ⓠ RS: p tbl / WS: k tbl

Ⓠ RS: k tbl / WS: p tbl

☐ repeat

PATTERN

Using yarn A, cast on 45 sts.

Join in other colours as needed.

Work Rows 1 to 63 of chart.

Bind (cast) off all sts using yarn A.

Weave in ends and block to finished size.

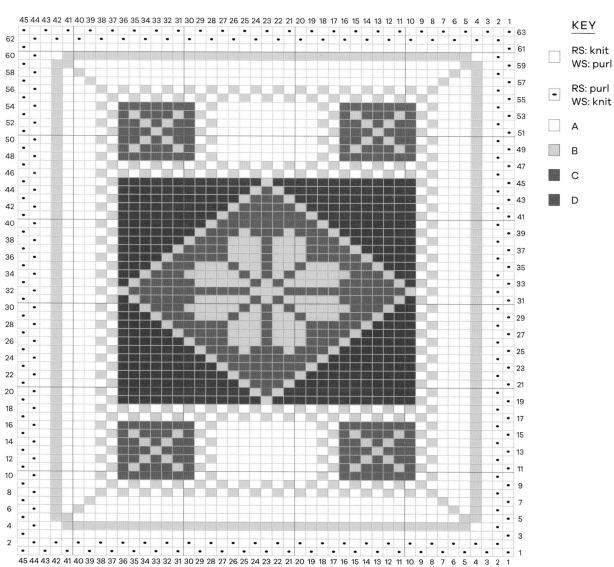

KEY

☐	RS: knit WS: purl
⊡	RS: purl WS: knit
☐	A
▨	B
▨	C
▨	D

NORDIC TREES

DESIGNER: KARIE WESTERMANN

YARN

A - Cream (Toulouse 030)

B - Dark Green (Karachi 016)

NEEDLES

US size 2 (2.75mm) DPNs, or as needed to achieve gauge (tension)

ACCESSORIES

4 stitch markers, including one distinct for BOR

GAUGE (TENSION)

24 sts x 42 rounds = 4 x 4in (10 x 10cm) square

FINISHED SIZE

7 x 7in (18 x 18cm)

NOTES

This tile is worked in the round from the outer edge to the centre.

When working the chart, the colour not in use should be stranded loosely across the back of the colour being used (see Techniques: Stranded Colourwork).

PATTERN

Using yarn A, cast on 176 sts. Join to work in the round, being careful not to twist the sts.

Knit 1 round.

Purl 1 round.

Next Round: *K44, place marker; rep from * three more times, with final marker for BOR.

Next Round: *P1, p2tog, p39, p2tog tbl, slip marker; rep from * three more times. 168 sts

Join in yarn B.

Repeating chart four times in each round, work Rows 1 to 38 of chart, decreasing before and after markers on rounds as indicated. 16 sts

Cut yarn A and continue with yarn B only.

Next Row: [K2tog] eight times, removing all markers. 8 sts

Cut yarn B and thread end through remaining sts, pulling tight to close the hole.

Weave in ends and block to finished size.

KEY

- ☐ knit
- ◿ k2tog
- ◺ ssk
- ☐ A
- ■ B

GRAPHENE

DESIGNER: ANNA NIKIPIROWICZ

YARN

Orange (Liverpool 065)

NEEDLES

US size 4 (3.5mm) DPNs, or as needed to achieve gauge (tension)

ACCESSORIES

6 stitch markers, including one distinct for BOR

US size G-6 (4mm) crochet hook for cast on chain

GAUGE (TENSION)

28 sts x 36 rounds = 4 x 4in (10 x 10cm) square

FINISHED SIZE

6¼ x 5¼in (16 x 13.5cm)

NOTES

This tile is worked in the round from the centre to the outer edge, starting with a crochet chain with stitches picked up in the chain to create the centre hole. Use the working yarn throughout.

PATTERN

Using crochet hook, make 19 chains and cut yarn. Leaving a long tail, pick up and knit 18 sts in WS of crochet chain. Join to work in the round, being careful not to twist the sts. Mark the beginning of the round. 18 sts

Round 1: [K3, yo, place marker] six times, with final marker for BOR.

Round 2 and following even-numbered rounds to Round 14: [Knit to 1 st before marker, k1 tbl, slip marker] six times.

Round 3: [Yo, k3, yo, k1 tbl, slip marker] six times. 36 sts

Round 5: [Yo, k5, yo, k1 tbl, slip marker] six times. 48 sts

Round 7: [Yo, k7, yo, k1 tbl, slip marker] six times. 60 sts

Round 9: [Yo, k9, yo, k1 tbl, slip marker] six times. 72 sts

Round 11: [Yo, k11, yo, k1 tbl, slip marker] six times. 84 sts

Round 13: [Yo, k13, yo, k1 tbl, slip marker] six times. 96 sts

Round 15: [Yo, k15, yo, k1 tbl, slip marker] six times. 108 sts

Round 16: [K7, yo, sk2p, yo, k7, k1 tbl] six times.

Round 17: [Yo, k17, yo, k1 tbl, slip marker] six times. 120 sts

Round 18: [K7, yo, k1, sk2p, k1, yo, k7, k1 tbl] six times.

Round 19: [Yo, k19, yo, k1 tbl, slip marker] six times. 132 sts

Round 20: [K7, yo, k2, sk2p, k2, yo, k7, k1 tbl] six times.

Round 21: [Yo, k21, yo, k1 tbl, slip marker] six times. 144 sts

Round 22: [K7, yo, k3, sk2p, k3, yo, k7, k1 tbl] six times.

Round 23: [Yo, k23, yo, k1 tbl, slip marker] six times. 156 sts

Bind (cast) off all sts.

Using working yarn cast-on yarn tail, join centre crochet chains to form a neat circle. Weave in ends and block to finished size.

ARC

· · · · · · ·

DESIGNER: ANNI HOWARD

YARN

A - Cream (Lyon 078)

B - Blue (Lahore 014)

NEEDLES

US size 3 (3.25mm) needles, or as
needed to achieve gauge (tension)

GAUGE (TENSION)

34 sts x 64 rows = 4 x 4in (10 x 10cm)
square

FINISHED SIZE

6 x 6in (15 x 15cm)

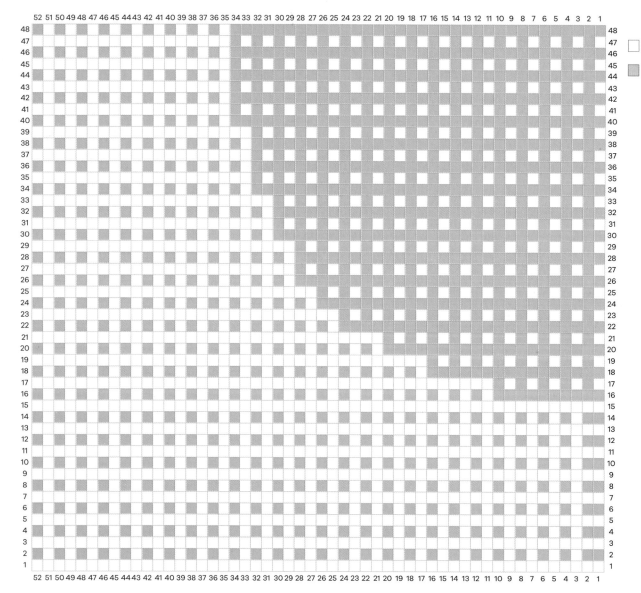

KEY

☐ A

▨ B

NOTES

Work this tile using mosaic knitting (see Techniques: Mosaic Knitting). Each chart row represents one RS row and one WS row. Knit sts that are the colour of the first st of the row, and slip the other colour.

PATTERN

Using yarn A, cast on 52 sts.

Work from chart as follows:

Row 1 (RS): Using yarn A, knit to end.

Row 1 (WS): Using yarn A, knit to end.

Row 2 (RS): Using yarn B, k2, *slip 1 purlwise, k1; rep from * to end.

Row 2 (WS): Using yarn B, *k1, move yarn to front, slip 1 purlwise, move yarn to back; rep from * to last 2 sts, k2.

Continue working from chart until Row 48 WS has been completed.

Bind (cast) off all sts knitwise using yarn B.

Weave in ends and block to finished size.

SASHIKO

DESIGNER: LISA MCFETRIDGE

YARN

A - Pink (Montreal 059)

B - Pale Lavender (Taipei 006)

NEEDLES

US size 2 (2.75mm) needles, or as needed to achieve gauge (tension)

GAUGE (TENSION)

34 sts x 38 rows = 4 x 4in (10 x 10cm) square

FINISHED SIZE

6 x 6¼in (15 x 16cm)

NOTES

Strand the colour not in use loosely across the back of the colour being used (see Techniques: Stranded Colourwork).

Knit the first and last stitch of every row whether on a RS or WS row, in order to create a tight edge.

PATTERN

Using yarn A, cast on 53 sts.

Join in yarn B as needed.

Work Rows 1 to 57 of chart.

Bind (cast) off all sts firmly purlwise
using yarn A.

Weave in ends and block to finished size.

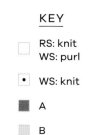

REGAL RHYTHM

DESIGNER: ASHLEIGH WEMPE

YARN

A - Medium Orange (Sevilla 076)

B - Dark Orange (Mexico City 075)

C - Light Grey (Cota 024)

D - Dark Blue (Bucharest 001)

E - Navy Blue (Philadelphia 007)

NEEDLES

US size 8 (5mm) DPNs

US size 7 (4.5mm) DPNs, or as needed to achieve gauge (tension)

ACCESSORIES

4 stitch markers, including one distinct for BOR

GAUGE (TENSION)

15 sts x 27 rounds = 4 x 4in (10 x 10cm) square using yarn held double on US size 7 (4.5mm) needles

FINISHED SIZE

7 x 7in (18 x 18cm)

NOTES

This tile is worked in the round from the outer edge to the centre. The yarn is held double throughout. Use two separate balls or find both ends of the ball. There is no border and the stockinette (stocking) stitch fabric will tend to roll even after blocking, so this design is intended to be part of a larger project.

When working the chart, the colour not in use should be stranded loosely across the back of the colour being used (see Techniques: Stranded Colourwork).

PATTERN

Using US size 8 (5mm) DPNs, and with one strand of yarn A and one strand of yarn B held together, cast on 108 sts.

Join to work in the round, being careful not to twist the sts.

Cut yarns A and B.

Change to US size 7 (4.5mm) DPNs.

Using two strands of yarn C as MC and one strand of yarn D together with one strand of yarn E as CC, work as follows:

Round 1: [Work Row 1 of chart, place marker] four times, with final marker for BOR.

Continue working as set, slipping markers and working decreases as shown, until chart is complete. 12 sts

Cut all yarn strands and thread CC tail through remaining sts, pulling tight to close the hole.

Weave in ends and block to finished size.

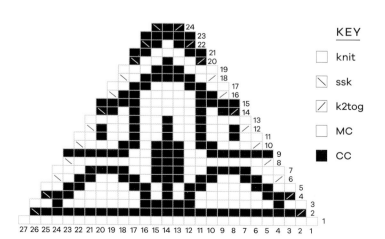

KEY

☐ knit

◻ ssk

◿ k2tog

☐ MC

■ CC

BANK VAULT

DESIGNER: ARELLA SEATON

YARN

A - Yellow (Brasov 038)

B - Black (Cairo 070)

NEEDLES

US size 2.5 (3mm) needles, or as
needed to achieve gauge (tension)

GAUGE (TENSION)

31 sts x 60 rows = 4 x 4in (10 x 10cm)
square

FINISHED SIZE

6 x 6in (15 x 15cm)

KEY

 A

 B

NOTES

Work this tile using mosaic knitting (see Techniques: Mosaic Knitting). Each chart row represents one RS row and one WS row. Knit sts that are the colour of the first st of the row, and slip the other colour.

PATTERN

Using yarn A, cast on 47 sts.

Work from chart as follows:

Row 1 (RS): Using yarn A, knit to end.

Row 1 (WS): Using yarn A, knit to end.

Row 2 (RS): Using yarn B, k1, *[slip 1 purlwise, k1] twice, slip 1 purlwise, k3, [slip 1 purlwise, k1] four times, slip 1 purlwise, k3; rep from * once more, [slip 1 purlwise, k1] three times.

Row 2 (WS): Using yarn B, k1, *[move yarn to front, slip 1 purlwise, move yarn to back, k1] twice, move yarn to front, slip 1 purlwise, move yarn to back, k3, [move yarn to front, slip 1 purlwise, move yarn to back, k1] four times, move yarn to front, slip 1 purlwise, move yarn to back, k3; rep from * once more, [move yarn to front, slip 1 purlwise, move yarn to back, k1] three times.

Continue working from chart until Row 45 WS has been completed.

Bind (cast) off all sts knitwise using yarn A.

Weave in ends and block to finished size.

THROUGH

DESIGNER: JOANNE FOWLER

YARN
Light Grey (Cota 024)

NEEDLES
US size 1.5 (2.5mm) DPNs, or as needed to achieve gauge (tension)

ACCESSORIES
5 stitch markers, including one distinct for BOR

GAUGE (TENSION)
21 sts x 44 rounds = 4 x 4in (10 x 10cm) square

FINISHED SIZE
6 x 6in (15 x 15cm)

NOTES

This tile is worked in the round from the centre out. Textured bands of garter stitch and eyelets alternate with stockinette (stocking) stitch bands.

Four markers indicate the start of the corners of the square, where increases shape the work on odd-numbered rounds. When not mentioned, slip all markers as you go.

PATTERN

Cast on 1 st, place marker, [cast on 2 sts, place marker] three times, cast on 1 st. Join to work in the round. Mark the beginning of the round. 8 sts

Round 1: [K1, yo, slip marker, k1, yo] four times. 16 sts

Round 2: Knit.

Round 3: [Knit to marker, yo, slip marker, k1, yo] four times, knit to end of round. 8 sts increased

Round 4: Knit.

Rounds 5 to 9: Rep Rounds 3 and 4 twice, then rep Round 3 once more.

Round 10: Purl.

Round 11: Rep Round 3.

Round 12: [*Yo, k2tog; rep from * to 1 st before marker, k4] four times, **yo, k2tog; rep from ** to end of round.

Round 13: Rep Round 3.

Round 14: Purl.

Rounds 15 to 26: Rep Rounds 3 to 14.

Round 27: Rep Round 3.

Round 28: Knit.

Round 29: Rep Round 3.

Round 30: Purl.

Rounds 31 and 32: Rep Rounds 29 and 30. 136 sts

Bind (cast) off all sts as follows: *K2tog, slip st from RH to LH needle; rep from * until 1 st remains.

Fasten off, pulling yarn through last st.

Use the cast-on yarn tail to close the hole at the centre if needed.

Weave in ends and block to finished size.

ART DECO WINDOW

DESIGNER: LILY LANGMAN

YARN

A - Red (Naples 043)

B - Cream (Lyon 078)

C - Yellow (Brasov 038)

D - Teal Green (Pasay 022)

E - Blue (Washington 013)

NEEDLES

US size 1.5 (2.5mm) needles, or as needed to achieve gauge (tension)

GAUGE (TENSION)

29 sts x 45 rows = 4 x 4in (10 x 10cm) square

FINISHED SIZE

6¼ x 5¼in (16 x 13.5cm)

NOTES

This tile is knitted with a border of garter stitch on the top and bottom edges and 2 garter stitches on each side. The chart is worked in stockinette (stocking) stitch.

When working with two or three colours at once, the colours not in use should be stranded loosely across the back of the colour being used (see Techniques: Stranded Colourwork).

When stranding the yarn becomes difficult, use a separate ball of yarn for each colour and twist the yarn about to be used around the colour just used to link yarns together on WS to avoid a hole (see Techniques: Intarsia).

PATTERN

Using yarn A, cast on 45 sts.

Work 4 rows of garter stitch.

Join in other colours as needed and work as follows:

Row 1 (RS): K2 using yarn A, knit Row 1 of chart, k2 using yarn A.

Row 2: K2 using A, purl Row 2 of chart, k2 using yarn A.

Keeping first 2 sts and last 2 sts in garter stitch using yarn A throughout, continue until chart is complete.

Cut all colours except yarn A.

Work 4 rows of garter stitch.

Bind (cast) off all sts.

Weave in ends and block to finished size.

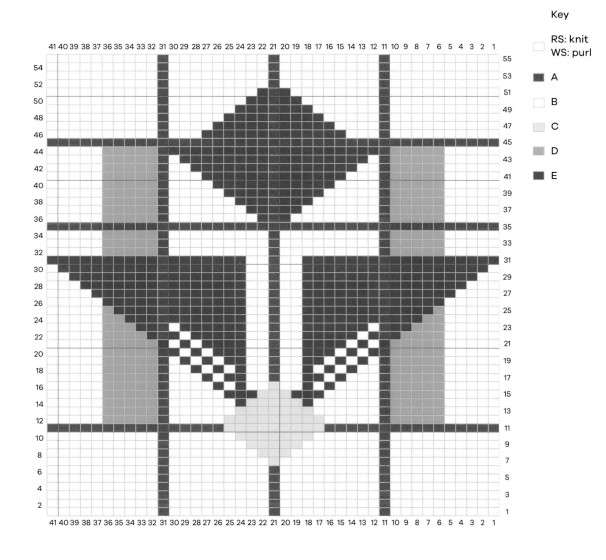

Key

RS: knit
WS: purl

■ A

□ B

▨ C

▨ D

■ E

OLD BLUE

DESIGNER: ANNAPLEXIS

YARN

A - Navy Blue (Philadelphia 007)

B - Pale Yellow (Delhi 039)

NEEDLES

US size 1.5 (2.5mm) needles, or as
needed to achieve gauge (tension)

GAUGE (TENSION)

29 sts x 45 rows = 4 x 4in (10 x 10cm) square

FINISHED SIZE

6¼ x 5½in (16 x 14cm)

NOTES

This tile is knitted with a border of garter stitch on
the top and bottom edges and 4 garter stitches
on each side. The chart is worked in stockinette
(stocking) stitch.

When working with two colours at once, the
colour not in use should be stranded loosely
across the back of the colour being used (see
Techniques: Stranded Colourwork).

Slip the first st of each row purlwise.

PATTERN

Using yarn A, cast on 45 sts.

Next Row: Slip 1, knit to end.

Rep this row four more times.

Join in yarn B and work as follows:

Row 1 (RS): Slip 1, k3 using yarn A,
knit Row 1 of chart, k4 using yarn A.

Row 2: Slip 1, k3 using yarn A, purl
Row 2 of chart, k4 using yarn A.

Keeping first 4 sts and last 4 sts in
garter stitch as set using yarn A
throughout, continue until chart
is complete.

Cut yarn B and continue with
yarn A only.

Next Row: Slip 1, knit to end.

Rep this row five more times.

Bind (cast) off all sts.

Weave in ends and block to
finished size.

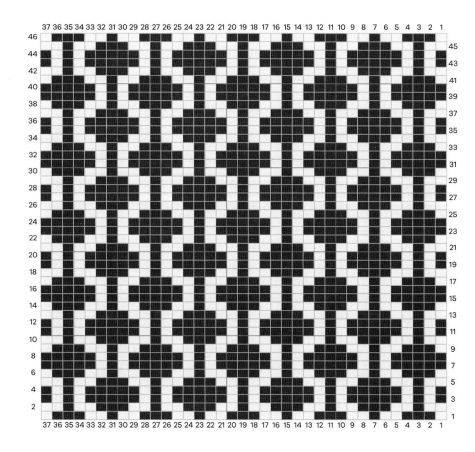

KEY

☐ RS: knit
WS: purl

■ A

☐ B

FRAZIL

DESIGNER: ANNIKEN ALLIS

YARN

A - Pale Lavender (Taipei 006)

B - Indigo Blue (Dallas 003)

NEEDLES

US size 4 (3.5mm) needles, or as needed to achieve gauge (tension)

GAUGE (TENSION)

28.5 sts x 61 rows = 4 x 4in (10 x 10cm) square

FINISHED SIZE

6 x 6¼in (15 x 16cm)

NOTES

Work this tile using mosaic knitting (see Techniques: Mosaic Knitting). Each chart row represents one RS row and one WS row. Knit stitches that are the colour of the first stitch of the row, and slip the other colour.

PATTERN

Using yarn A, cast on 43 sts.

Knit 1 row.

Work from chart as follows:

Row 1 (RS): Using yarn A, k1, slip 1 purlwise, k1, *[k2, slip 1 purlwise] twice, k1, slip 1 purlwise, k2, slip 1 purlwise, k1; rep from * twice more, k2, slip 1 purlwise, k1.

Row 1 (WS): Using yarn A, k1, move yarn to front, slip 1 purlwise, move yarn to back, k2, *k1, move yarn to front, slip 1 purlwise, move yarn to back, k2, move yarn to front, slip 1 purlwise, move yarn to back, k1, [move yarn to front, slip 1 purlwise, move yarn to back, k2] twice; rep from * twice more, k1, move yarn to front, slip 1 purlwise, move yarn to back, k1.

Row 2 (RS): Using yarn B, k3, *[slip 1 purlwise, k2] four times; rep from * to twice more, slip 1 purlwise, k3.

Row 2 (WS): Using yarn B, k3, move yarn to front, slip 1 purlwise, move yarn to back, *[k2, move yarn to front, slip 1 purlwise, move yarn to back] four times; rep from * twice more, k3.

Continue working from chart until complete, rep Rows 1 to 18 once more, then rep Rows 1 to 12 only once again.

Cut yarn B and continue with yarn A only.

Knit 1 row.

Bind (cast) off all sts knitwise.

Weave in ends and block to finished size.

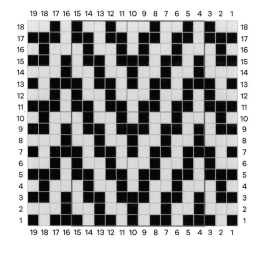

KEY

□ A

■ B

□ repeat

CLOVER

DESIGNER: CARMEN JORISSEN

YARN

A - Pink (Tokyo 061)

B - Burgundy (Bogotá 050)

NEEDLES

US size 2.5 (3mm) needles, or as needed to achieve gauge (tension)

GAUGE (TENSION)

31 sts x 30 rows = 4 x 4in (10 x 10cm) square

FINISHED SIZE

5¾ x 5¾in (14.5 x 14.5cm)

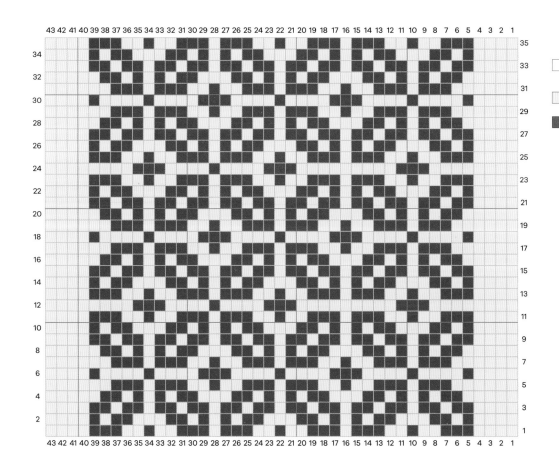

KEY

☐ RS: knit
WS: purl

▨ A

▨ B

NOTES

This tile is worked in stockinette (stocking) stitch following the colourwork chart. The colour not in use should be stranded loosely across the back of the colour being used (see Techniques: Stranded Colourwork).

To make your colourwork look neat, wrap yarn B at the start of every row, preferably on the second stitch, as follows:

On RS rows, insert RH needle into next stitch (to be worked in yarn A), lay yarn B horizontally from right to left over RH needle, knit the stitch using yarn A. Yarn B is now wrapped. Make sure yarn B is not being pulled through the stitch.

On WS rows, insert RH needle into next stitch (to be worked in yarn A), hold yarn B up so that it lays vertically across RH needle, purl the stitch using yarn A.

PATTERN

Using yarn A, cast on 43 sts.

Set-Up Row (WS): Using yarn A, purl to end.

Next Row: Using yarn A, knit.

Next Row: Using yarn A, purl.

Join in yarn B.

Work Rows 1 to 35 of chart.

Cut yarn B and continue with yarn A only.

Next Row (WS): Purl to end.

Next Row: Knit.

Next Row: Purl.

Bind (cast) off all sts.

Weave in ends and block to finished size.

GRAVITATIONAL WAVES

DESIGNER: ARELLA SEATON

YARN

A - Dark Blue (Bucharest 001)

B - Yellow (Brasov 038)

C - Cream (Lyon 078)

NEEDLES

US size 2.5 (3mm) DPNs, or as needed to achieve gauge (tension)

ACCESSORIES

4 stitch markers, including one distinct for BOR

GAUGE (TENSION)

26 sts x 50 rounds = 4 x 4in (10 x 10cm) square

FINISHED SIZE

8 x 8in (20 x 20cm)

NOTES

This tile is worked in the round from the centre to the outer edge, with only one colour worked in each round. Slip all sts purlwise with yarn stranded loosely across the back of the work.

SPECIAL ABBREVIATIONS

Rli: right lifted increase – lift the RH leg of st below next st on LH needle onto LH needle and knit it

Lli: left lifted increase – lift the LH leg of st 2 rows below st on RH needle onto LH needle and knit it through the back loop

PATTERN

Using yarn A, cast on 12 sts using a centre-out cast-on method (see Techniques: Centre-Out Cast On) or cast on with your preferred method, leaving a long yarn tail. Join to work in the round, being careful not to twist the sts. Mark the beginning of the round. 12 sts

Set-Up Round: [K3, place marker] four times, with final marker for BOR.

Repeating chart four times in each round, work Rows 1 to 50 of chart, increasing before and after markers on odd-numbered rounds as indicated and joining in yarns as required. 212 sts

Cut all yarns except yarn A.

Bind (cast) off all sts.

Use the cast-on yarn tail to close the hole at the centre if needed. Weave in ends and block to finished size.

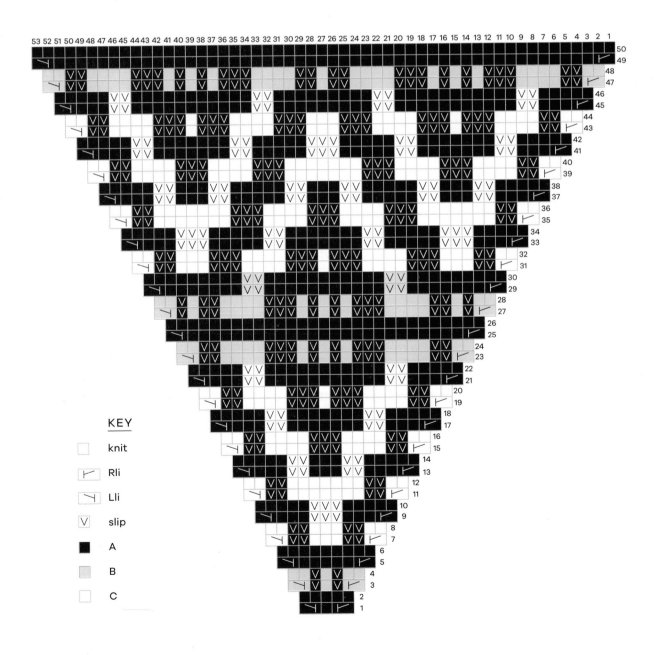

KEY

☐	knit
⊢	Rli
⊣	Lli
V	slip
◼	A
▨	B
☐	C

FOLIAGE

DESIGNER: ANNA NIKIPIROWICZ

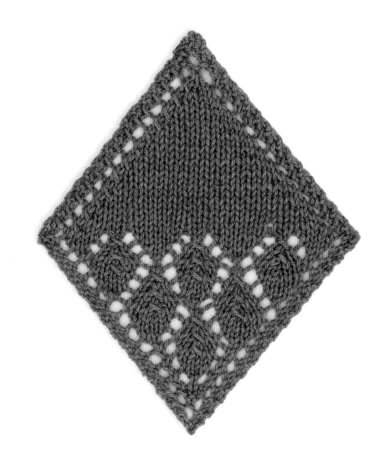

YARN

Teal Green (Suwon 018)

NEEDLES

US size 4 (3.5mm) needles, or as needed to achieve gauge (tension)

GAUGE (TENSION)

24 sts x 42 rows = 4 x 4in (10 x 10cm) square

FINISHED SIZE

Point to point: 5½ x 5½in (14 x 14cm)

NOTES

This tile is worked from one corner to the other with increases and the lace pattern to the centre point, then decreases to shape the second half, which is in stockinette (stocking) stitch between the edging. You can block the finished diamond to a more traditional square shape if you prefer.

PATTERN

Cast on 4 sts.

INCREASE/LACE SECTION

Row 1 (WS): Knit.

Row 2 (RS): K2, yo, k2. 5 sts

Row 3: Knit.

Row 4: K2, yo, k1, yo, k2. 7 sts

Row 5: Knit.

Row 6: K2, yo, k3, yo, k2. 9 sts

Row 7 and following WS rows to Row 31: K2, purl to last 2 sts, k2.

Row 8: K2, yo, k2tog, yo, k1, yo, skpo, yo, k2. 11 sts

Row 10: K2, yo, k2tog, yo, k3, yo, skpo, yo, k2. 13 sts

Row 12: K2, yo, k2tog, yo, k5, yo, skpo, yo, k2. 15 sts

Row 14: K2, [yo, k2] twice, sk2p, [k2, yo] twice, k2. 17 sts

Row 16: K2, yo, k4, yo, k1, sk2p, k1, yo, k4, yo, k2. 19 sts

Row 18: K2, yo, k6, yo, sk2p, yo, k6, yo, k2. 21 sts

Row 20: K2, yo, [k1, yo, k2, sk2p, k2, yo] twice, k1, yo, k2. 23 sts

Row 22: K2, yo, [k3, yo, k1, sk2p, k1, yo] twice, k3, yo, k2. 25 sts

Row 24: K2, yo, [k5, yo, sk2p, yo] twice, k5, yo, k2. 27 sts

Row 26: K2, yo, k3, k2tog, k2, yo, k1, yo, k2, sk2p, k2, yo, k1, yo, k2, skpo, k3, yo, k2. 29 sts

Row 28: K2, yo, k2, [yo, k1, sk2p, k1, yo, k3] twice, yo, k1, sk2p, k1, yo, k2, yo, k2. 31 sts

Row 30: K2, yo, k4, [yo, sk2p, yo, k5] twice, yo, sk2p, yo, k4, yo, k2. 33 sts

DECREASE SECTION

Row 32 (RS): K1, k2tog, yo, k2tog, knit to last 5 sts, [ssk, yo] twice, k1. 2 sts decreased

Row 33 (WS): K2, purl to last 2 sts, k2.

Rows 34 to 55: Rep Rows 32 and 33 eleven times. 9 sts

Row 56: K1, k2tog, yo, k3tog, yo, ssk, k1. 7 sts

Row 57: Knit.

Row 58: K2, k2tog, yo, k3tog, k1. 5 sts

Row 59: Knit.

Row 60: K1, k3tog, k1. 3 sts

Bind (cast) off all sts.

Weave in ends and block to finished size.

SQUARE
THE CIRCLE

DESIGNER: KAROLINA ADAMCZYK

YARN

A - Burgundy (Bogotá 050)

B - Pink (Bangalore 052)

NEEDLES

US size 1.5 (2.5mm) DPNs, or as
needed to achieve gauge (tension)

ACCESSORIES

4 stitch markers, including one distinct
for BOR

GAUGE (TENSION)

29 sts x 38 rounds = 4 x 4in (10 x 10cm)
square

FINISHED SIZE

6½ x 6½in (16.5 x 16.5cm)

NOTES

*This tile is worked in the round from the
outer edge to the centre. It begins with
a ribbed border, with markers indicating
the corners of the square where
decreases shape the work.*

*The chart is repeated four times
in each round. When working the
chart, the colour not in use should be
stranded loosely across the back of
the colour being used (see Techniques:
Stranded Colourwork).*

PATTERN

Using yarn A, cast on 180 sts. Join to
work in the round, being careful not to
twist the sts.

Round 1: *[K1, p1] 22 times, k1, place
marker; rep from * three more times,
with the final marker for BOR.

Round 2: *Ssk, [k1, p1] 20 times, k1, k2tog,
slip marker; rep from * three more times.
172 sts

Round 3: *K1, [k1, p1] 20 times, k2, slip
marker; rep from * three more times.

Round 4: *Ssk, knit to 2 sts before
marker, k2tog, slip marker; rep from *
three more times. 164 sts

Join in yarn B.

Repeating chart four times in each
round, work Rows 1 to 25 of chart,
decreasing before and after markers on
rounds as indicated. 28 sts

Cut yarn B and continue with
yarn A only.

Next Round: Knit.

Next Round: [K2tog] 14 times, removing
all markers. 14 sts

Cut yarn A and thread end through
remaining sts, pulling tight to
close the hole.

Weave in ends and block to finished size.

KEY

☐ knit

◥ ssk

◢ k2tog

■ A

■ B

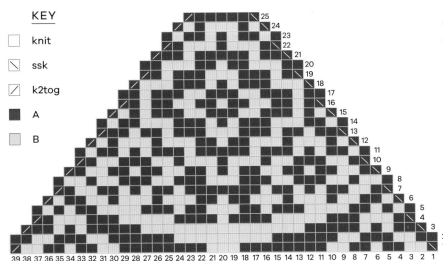

ARGYLE

· · · · · · · · · · · · · · ·

DESIGNER: ASHLEY GIBBONS

YARN

Green (Abu Dhabi 032)

NEEDLES

US size 2 (2.75mm) needles, or as needed to achieve gauge (tension)

ACCESSORIES

2 stitch markers

GAUGE (TENSION)

30 sts x 40 rows = 4 x 4in (10 x 10cm) square

FINISHED SIZE

5¼ x 5¼in (13.5 x 13.5cm)

NOTES

This tile uses only knit and purl stitches to create a textured pattern. Slip the first stitch of each row purlwise.

PATTERN

Cast on 42 sts.

Rows 1 to 3: Slip 1, knit to end.

Row 4 (WS): Slip 1, k2, place marker, [k1, p1, k3, p1, k1, p5] three times, place marker, k3.

Row 5: Slip 1, k2, slip marker, [k5, p1, k1, p3, k1, p1] three times, slip marker, k3.

Row 6: Slip 1, k2, slip marker, [k2, p1, k1, p1, k3, p3, k1] three times, slip marker, k3.

Row 7: Slip 1, k2, slip marker, [p1, k3, p3, k1, p1, k1, p2] three times, slip marker, k3.

Row 8: Slip 1, k2, slip marker, [k3, p1, k5, p1, k2] three times, slip marker, k3.

Row 9: Slip 1, k2, slip marker, [p2, k1, p5, k1, p3] three times, slip marker, k3.

Row 10: Slip 1, k2, slip marker, [k2, p3, k3, p1, k1, p1, k1] three times, slip marker, k3.

Row 11: Slip 1, k2, slip marker, [p1, k1, p1, k1, p3, k3, p2] three times, slip marker, k3.

Row 12: Slip 1, k2, slip marker, [k1, p5, k1, p1, k3, p1] three times, slip marker, k3.

Row 13: Slip 1, k2, slip marker, [k1, p3, k1, p1, k5, p1] three times, slip marker, k3.

Row 14: Slip 1, k2, slip marker, [p7, k5] three times, slip marker, k3.

Row 15: Slip 1, k2, slip marker, [p5, k7] three times, slip marker, k3.

Row 16: Slip 1, k2, slip marker, [k1, p5, k1, p1, k3, p1] three times, slip marker, k3.

Row 17: Slip 1, k2, slip marker, [k1, p3, k1, p1, k5, p1] three times, slip marker, k3.

Rows 18 and 19: Rep Rows 10 and 11.

Rows 20 and 21: Rep Rows 8 and 9.

Rows 22 and 23: Rep Rows 6 and 7.

Rows 24 and 25: Rep Rows 4 and 5.

Row 26: Slip 1, k2, slip marker, [p1, k5, p6] three times, slip marker, k3.

Row 27: Slip 1, k2, slip marker, [k6, p5, k1] three times, slip marker, k3.

Rows 28 to 39: Rep Rows 4 to 15.

Rows 40 and 41: Rep Rows 12 and 13.

Rows 42 and 43: Rep Rows 10 and 11.

Rows 44 and 45: Rep Rows 8 and 9.

Rows 46 and 47: Rep Rows 6 and 7.

Rows 48 and 49: Rep Rows 4 and 5.

Rows 50 and 51: Rep Rows 26 and 27.

Rows 52 to 54: Rep Rows 1 to 3.

Bind (cast) off all sts knitwise.

Weave in ends and block to finished size.

LOVE PUNCH

DESIGNER: LYNNE ROWE

YARN

Pink (Bangalore 052)

NEEDLES

US size 2.5 (3mm) needles, or as needed to achieve gauge (tension)

GAUGE (TENSION)

30 sts x 43 rows = 4 x 4in (10 x 10cm) square

FINISHED SIZE

6 x 6in (15 x 15cm)

NOTES

The heart motif is worked in seed (moss) st and outlined with eyelets formed from yarn overs on a stockinette (stocking) stitch background.

PATTERN

Cast on 43 sts.

Row 1 (RS): Knit.

Row 2: Purl.

Rows 3 to 14: Rep Rows 1 and 2 six times.

Row 15: K21, yo, k2tog, k20.

Row 16: Purl.

Row 17: K19, yo, k2tog, p1, skpo, yo, k19.

Row 18: P20, k1, p1, k1, p20.

Row 19: K18, yo, k2tog, k1, p1, k1, skpo, yo, k18.

Row 20: Rep Row 18.

Row 21: K17, yo, k2tog, [p1, k1] twice, p1, skpo, yo, k17.

Row 22: P18, [k1, p1] three times, k1, p18.

Row 23: K16, yo, k2tog, [k1, p1] three times, k1, skpo, yo, k16.

Row 24: Rep Row 22.

Row 25: K15, yo, k2tog, [p1, k1] four times, p1, skpo, yo, k15.

Row 26: P16, [k1, p1] five times, k1, p16.

Row 27: K14, yo, k2tog, [p1, k1] five times, k1, skpo, yo, k14.

Row 28: Rep Row 26.

Row 29: K13, yo, k2tog, [p1, k1] six times, p1, skpo, yo, k13.

Row 30: P14, [k1, p1] seven times, k1, p14.

Row 31: K12, yo, k2tog, [k1, p1] seven times, k1, skpo, yo, k12.

Row 32: Rep Row 30.

Row 33: K11, yo, k2tog, [p1, k1] eight times, p1, skpo, yo, k11.

Row 34: P12, [k1, p1] nine times, k1, p12.

Row 35: K10, yo, k2tog, [k1, p1] nine times, k1, skpo, yo, k10.

Row 36: Rep Row 34.

Row 37: K9, yo, k2tog, [p1, k1] ten times, p1, skpo, yo, k9.

Row 38: P10, [k1, p1] 11 times, k1, p10.

Row 39: K8, yo, k2tog, [k1, p1] 11 times, k1, skpo, yo, k8.

Row 40: Rep Row 38.

Row 41: K11, [p1, k1] ten times, p1, k11.

Row 42: Rep Row 38.

Row 43: K8, yo, k2tog, [k1, p1] five times, k1, yo, k2tog, [p1, k1] five times, skpo, yo, k8.

Row 44: P10, [k1, p1] four times, k1, p5, [k1, p1] four times, k1, p10.

Row 45: K9, yo, k2tog, [p1, k1] four times, yo, k2tog, k1, skpo, yo, [k1, p1] four times, skpo, yo, k9.

Row 46: P12, [k1, p1] twice, k1, p9, [k1, p1] twice, k1, p12.

Row 47: K10, yo, k2tog, [k1, p1] three times, yo, k2tog, k3, skpo, yo, [k1, p1] three times, skpo, yo, k10.

Row 48: Rep Row 46.

Row 49: K11, [yo, k2tog, k1] twice, yo, k2tog, k5, [skpo, yo, k1] twice, skpo, yo, k11.

Row 50: Purl.

Row 51: Knit.

Rows 52 to 63: Rep Rows 50 and 51 six times.

Bind (cast) off all sts knitwise.

Weave in ends and block to finished size.

ROMANTIC MEDALLION

DESIGNER: ASHLEIGH WEMPE

YARN

A - Medium Orange (Sevilla 076)

B - Dark Orange (Mexico City 075)

C - Light Grey (Cota 024)

D - Dark Blue (Bucharest 001)

E - Navy Blue (Philadelphia 007)

NEEDLES

US size 8 (5mm) DPNs

US size 7 (4.5mm) DPNs, or as needed to achieve gauge (tension)

ACCESSORIES

4 stitch markers, including one distinct for BOR

GAUGE (TENSION)

15 sts x 27 rounds = 4 x 4in (10 x 10cm) square using yarn held double on US size 7 (4.5mm) needles

FINISHED SIZE

7 x 7in (18 x 18cm)

NOTES

This tile is worked in the round from the outer edge to the centre. The yarn is held double throughout. Use two separate balls or find both ends of the ball. There is no border and the stockinette (stocking) stitch fabric will tend to roll even after blocking, so this design is intended to be part of a larger project.

When working the chart, the colour not in use should be stranded loosely across the back of the colour being used (see Techniques: Stranded Colourwork).

PATTERN

Using US size 8 (5mm) DPNs, and with one strand of yarn A and one strand of yarn B held together, cast on 108 sts. Join to work in the round, being careful not to twist the sts.

Cut yarns A and B.

Change to US size 7 (4.5mm) DPNs.

Using two strands of yarn C as MC and one strand of yarn D together with one strand of yarn E as CC, work as follows:

Round 1: [Work Row 1 of chart, place marker] four times, with final marker for BOR.

Continue working as set, slipping markers and working decreases as shown, until chart is complete. 12 sts

Cut all yarn strands and thread MC tail through remaining sts, pulling tight to close the hole.

Weave in ends and block to finished size.

KEY

☐	knit
◹	k2tog
◺	ssk
☐	MC
■	CC

STARBURST

DESIGNER: SUZY RAI

YARN

A - Light Grey (Cota 024)

B - Brown (Toronto 063)

NEEDLES

US size 2.5 (3mm) needles, or as
needed to achieve gauge (tension)

GAUGE (TENSION)

30 sts x 40 rows = 4 x 4in (10 x 10cm)
square

FINISHED SIZE

5½ x 5½in (14 x 14cm)

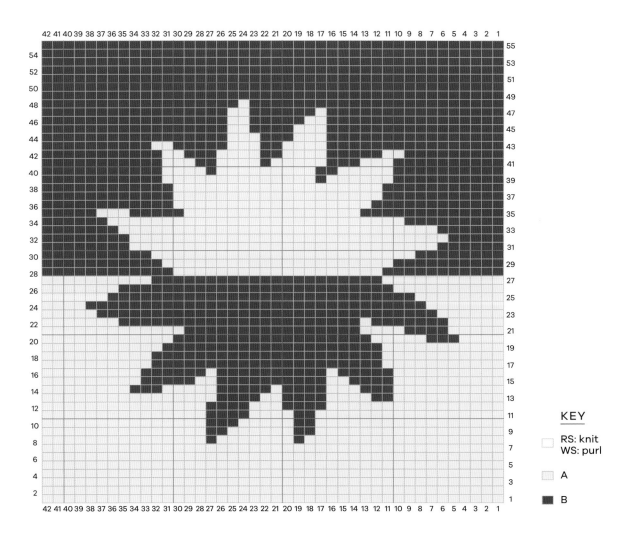

KEY

☐ RS: knit
WS: purl

▨ A

■ B

NOTES

The chart is worked in stockinette (stocking) stitch throughout.

When working with two or three colours at once, the colours not in use should be stranded loosely across the back of the colour being used (see Techniques: Stranded Colourwork).

When stranding the yarn becomes difficult, use a separate small ball of yarn for each colour and twist the yarns to avoid a hole (see Techniques: Intarsia).

PATTERN

Using yarn A, cast on 42 sts.

Join in yarn B as needed.

Work Rows 1 to 55 of chart.

Bind (cast) off all sts using yarn B.

Weave in ends and block to finished size.

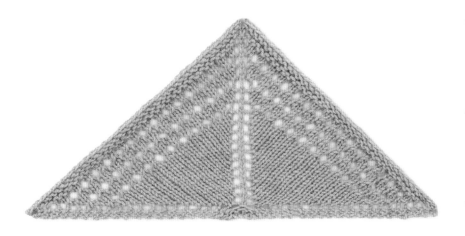

TRILATERAL

DESIGNER: ANNA NIKIPIROWICZ

YARN

Beige (Buenos Aires 067)

NEEDLES

US size 4 (3.5mm) needles, or as needed to achieve gauge (tension)

ACCESSORIES

Stitch marker for centre stitch

GAUGE (TENSION)

27 sts x 38 rows = 4 x 4in (10 x 10cm) square

FINISHED SIZE

7¾ x 4¾in (19.5 x 12cm)

NOTES

This tile is worked from the centre of the long bottom of the triangle to the top point, increasing at the edges and on each side of the centre stitch to shape. Mark the centre stitch in Row 5.

PATTERN

Cast on 7 sts.

Rows 1 to 4: Knit.

Row 5 (RS): K2, yo, k1, yo, k1 tbl (place marker in centre st), yo, k1, yo, k2. 11 sts

Row 6: K2, purl to last 2 sts, k2.

Row 7: K2, yo, knit to centre st, yo, k1 tbl, yo, knit to last 2 sts, k2. 4 sts increased

Rows 8 to 25: Rep Rows 6 and 7 nine times. 51 sts

Row 26 (WS): K2, purl to last 2 sts, k2.

Row 27: K2, yo, [k2tog, yo] to 1 st before centre st, k1, yo, k1 tbl (centre st), yo, k1, [yo, k2tog] to last 2 sts, yo, k2. 4 sts increased

Row 28: Rep Row 26.

Row 29: K2, yo, knit to centre st, yo, k1 tbl, yo, knit to last 2 sts, k2. 4 sts increased

Rows 30 to 37: Rep Rows 26 to 29 twice. 75 sts

Row 38: Rep Row 26.

Row 39: Rep Row 29. 79 sts

Row 40: Knit.

Row 41: Rep Row 29. 83 sts

Row 42: Knit.

Bind (cast) off using a stretchy method as follows: k2, *slip both sts back to LH needle, k2tog tbl, k1; rep from * to end.

Fasten off, pulling yarn through last st.

Weave in ends and block to finished size.

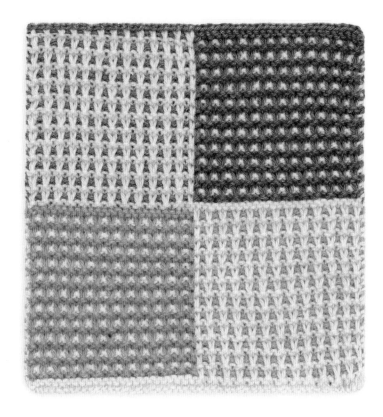

CORNERS

DESIGNER: ANNI HOWARD

YARN

A - Cream (Lyon 078)

B - Orange (Quebec 077)

C - Blue (Lahore 014)

NEEDLES

US size 3 (3.25mm) needles, or as needed to achieve gauge (tension)

GAUGE (TENSION)

34 sts x 64 rows = 4 x 4in (10 x 10cm) square

FINISHED SIZE

6 x 6in (15 x 15cm)

NOTES

Work this tile using mosaic knitting (see Techniques: Mosaic Knitting). Each chart row represents one RS row and one WS row. Knit stitches that are the colour of the first stitch of the row, and slip the other colour.

PATTERN

Using yarn A, cast on 52 sts.

Work from chart as follows:

Row 1 (RS): Using yarn A, knit to end.

Row 1 (WS): Using yarn A, knit to end.

Row 2 (RS): Using yarn B, [k1, slip 1 purlwise] 13 times, k26.

Row 2 (WS): Using yarn B, k26, [move yarn to front, slip 1 purlwise, move yarn to back, k1] 13 times.

Continue working from chart until Row 48 WS has been completed, cutting yarn B and joining yarn C after Row 25.

Bind (cast) off all sts knitwise using yarn C.

Weave in ends and block to finished size.

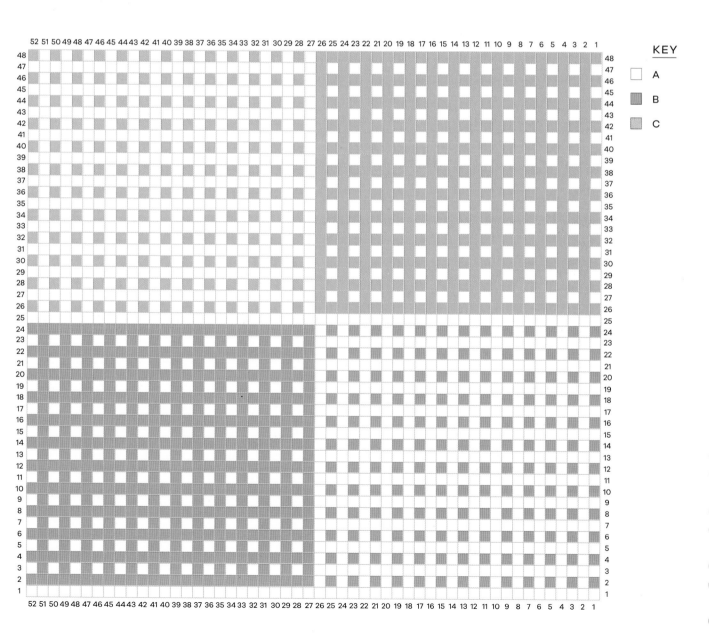

KEY

A
B
C

ANCHORED

DESIGNER: AZMIYA PADAVIA

YARN

A - Light Grey (Cota 024)

B - Blue (Kabul 004)

NEEDLES

US size 2.5 (3mm) needles, or as
needed to achieve gauge (tension)

GAUGE (TENSION)

30 sts x 30 rows = 4 x 4in (10 x 10cm) square

FINISHED SIZE

6¼ x 6¼in (16 x 16cm)

KEY

☐	RS: knit WS: purl
•	WS: knit
☐	A
■	B

NOTES

Strand the colour not in use loosely across the back of the colour being used (see Techniques: Stranded Colourwork).

Knit the first and last stitch of every row whether on a RS or WS row, in order to create a tight edge.

PATTERN

Using yarn A, cast on 47 sts.

Set-Up Row (WS): Using yarn A, purl to end.

Join in yarn B.

Work Rows 1 to 45 of chart.

Cut yarn B.

Next Row (WS): Using yarn A, purl to end.

Bind (cast) off all sts using yarn A.

Weave in ends and block to finished size.

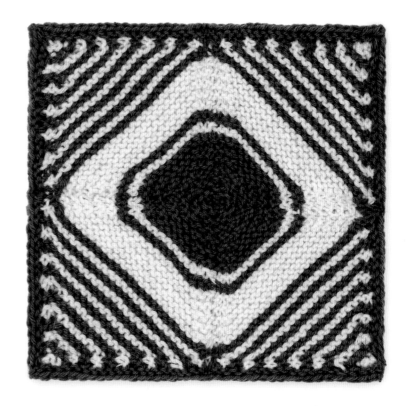

CORNISH POTTERY

DESIGNER: HELEN BIRCH

YARN
A - Cream (Lyon 078)

B - Blue (Boston 011)

NEEDLES
US size 2.5 (3mm) needles, or as needed to achieve gauge (tension)

GAUGE (TENSION)
28 sts x 56 rows = 4 x 4in (10 x 10cm) square

FINISHED SIZE
6 x 6in (15 x 15cm)

NOTES

This tile consists of four smaller striped squares that are sewn together before a border is picked up and worked along each side in turn.

PATTERN

STRIPED SQUARE (MAKE 4)

Using yarn A, cast on 2 sts.

Row 1 (RS): Using yarn A, kfb, k1. 3 sts

Row 2: Using yarn A, k3.

Row 3: Using yarn B, k1, (kfb) twice. 5 sts

Row 4: Using yarn B, k5.

Row 5: Using yarn A, k1, (kfb) twice, k2. 7 sts

Row 6: Using yarn A, k7.

Row 7: Using yarn B, k1, kfb, k2 kfb, k2. 9 sts

Row 8: Using yarn B, k9.

Row 9: Using yarn A, k1, kfb, knit to last 3 sts, kfb, k2. 2 sts increased

Row 10: Using yarn A, knit to end.

Row 11: Using yarn B, k1, kfb, knit to last 3 sts, kfb, k2. 2 sts increased

Row 12: Using yarn B, knit to end.

Rows 13 to 28: Rep Rows 9 to 12 four times. 29 sts

Row 29: Using yarn A, k2, skpo, knit to last 4 sts, k2tog, k2. 2 sts decreased

Row 30: Using yarn A, knit to end.

Rows 31 to 38: Rep Rows 29 and 30 four times. 19 sts

Row 39: Using yarn B, k2, skpo, knit to last 4 sts, k2tog, k2. 17 sts

Row 40: Using yarn B, knit to end.

Row 41: Using yarn A, k2, skpo, knit to last 4 sts, k2tog, k2. 15 sts

Row 42: Using yarn A, knit to end.

Cut yarn A and continue with yarn B only.

Row 43: K2, skpo, k to last 4 sts, k2tog, k2. 2 sts decreased

Row 44: Knit to end.

Rows 45 to 50: Rep Rows 43 and 44 three times. 7 sts

Row 51: K2, sl1, k2tog, psso, k2. 5 sts

Row 52: K5.

Row 53: K1, sk2p, k1. 3 sts

Row 54: K3.

Row 55: K1, skpo. 2 sts

Row 56: K2.

Row 57: K2tog.

Fasten off, pulling yarn through last st and leaving a long tail for sewing together.

Join your quarter tiles together with fasten-off points as centre.

BORDER

With RS facing and using yarn B, starting at one corner pick up and knit 40 sts along side edge to next corner, turn.

Next Row: K40, turn.

Bind (cast) off until 1 st remains on RH needle, do not turn.

**Pick up and knit 40 sts along next side edge to next corner. 41 sts

Next Row: K41, turn.

Bind (cast) off until 1 st remains on RH needle, do not turn. **

Rep from ** to ** twice more.

Fasten off, pulling yarn through last st.

FINISHING

Weave in ends and block to finished size.

YARN

A - Cream (Lyon 078)

B - Red (Naples 043)

C - Pink (Marrakech 051)

D - Dark Green (Karachi 016)

NEEDLES

US size 1.5 (2.5mm) needles, or as needed to achieve gauge (tension)

GAUGE (TENSION)

29 sts x 45 rows = 4 x 4in (10 x 10cm) square

FINISHED SIZE

7 x 5¾in (18 x 14.5cm)

NOTES

This tile is knitted with a border of garter stitch on the top and bottom edges and 3 garter stitches on each side. The chart is worked in stockinette (stocking) stitch.

When working with two or three colours at once, the colours not in use should be stranded loosely across the back of the colour being used (see Techniques: Stranded Colourwork).

When stranding the yarn becomes difficult, use a separate ball of yarn for each colour and twist the yarn about to be used around the colour just used to link yarns together on WS to avoid a hole (see Techniques: Intarsia).

If you prefer to work a smaller tile without the border, cast on 45 stitches using yarn D, work the chart, then bind (cast) off using yarn D.

PATTERN

Using yarn D, cast on 51 sts.

Work 4 rows of garter stitch.

Join in other colours as needed and work as follows:

Row 1 (RS): K3 using yarn D, knit Row 1 of chart, k3 using yarn D.

Row 2: K3 using yarn D, purl Row 2 of chart, k3 using yarn D.

Keeping first 3 sts and last 3 sts in garter stitch using yarn D throughout, continue until chart is complete.

Cut all colours except yarn D.

Work 3 rows of garter stitch.

Bind (cast) off all sts.

Weave in ends and block to finished size.

KEY

☐	RS: knit / WS: purl
☐	A
▨	B
▨	C
■	D

FORMAL GARDEN

DESIGNER: ARELLA SEATON

YARN

A - Light Blue (Ulsan 015)

B - Dark Blue (Bucharest 001)

NEEDLES

US size 2.5 (3mm) needles, or as
needed to achieve gauge (tension)

GAUGE (TENSION)

31 sts x 60 rows = 4 x 4in (10 x 10cm) square

FINISHED SIZE

6 x 6in (15 x 15cm)

KEY

A

B

NOTES

Work this tile using mosaic knitting (see Techniques: Mosaic Knitting). Each chart row represents one RS row and one WS row. Knit stitches that are the colour of the first stitch of the row, and slip the other colour.

PATTERN

Using yarn A, cast on 47 sts.

Work from chart as follows:

Row 1 (RS): Using yarn A, knit to end.

Row 1 (WS): Using yarn A, knit to end.

Row 2 (RS): Using yarn B, k1, *slip 1 purlwise, k1; rep from * to end.

Row 2 (WS): Using yarn B, k1, *move yarn to front, slip 1 purlwise, move yarn to back, k1; rep from * to end.

Continue working from chart until Row 45 WS has been completed.

Bind (cast) off all sts knitwise using yarn A.

Weave in ends and block to finished size.

CAMELLIA

DESIGNER: ANNIKEN ALLIS

YARN

Pale Lavender (Taipei 006)

NEEDLES

US size 4 (3.5mm) DPNs, or as needed to achieve gauge (tension)

ACCESSORIES

4 stitch markers, including one distinct for BOR

GAUGE (TENSION)

20 sts x 37.5 rounds = 4 x 4in (10 x 10cm) square

FINISHED SIZE

Without garter stitch edging: 6¼ x 6¼in (16 x 16cm)

With garter stitch edging: 7 x 7in (18 x 18cm)

NOTES

This tile is worked in the round from the centre out. Yarn overs are worked before and after the corners on odd-numbered rounds for shaping.

Rounds 1 to 16 are also shown in the chart and are worked four times in each round. Work an additional 8-stitch repeat in each subsequent repeat of Rounds 9 to 16.

The garter stitch edging is optional.

PATTERN

Cast on 8 sts. Join to work in the round being careful not to twist stitches. Mark the beginning of the round.

Next Round: Knit.

Round 1: *[Yo, k1] twice, place marker; rep from * three more times, with final marker for BOR. 16 sts

Round 2: [Knit to marker, slip marker] four times.

Round 3: [Yo, k3, yo, k1] four times. 24 sts

Round 4: [Knit to marker, slip marker] four times.

Round 5: [Yo, k5, yo, k1] four times. 32 sts

Round 6: [Knit to marker, slip marker] four times.

Round 7: [Yo, k7, yo, k1] four times. 40 sts

Round 8: [Knit to marker, slip marker] four times.

Round 9: [Yo, *k1, yo, ssk, k3, k2tog, yo; rep from * to 2 sts before marker, k1, yo, k1, slip marker] four times. 8 sts increased

Round 10: [Knit to marker, slip marker] four times.

Round 11: [Yo, k1, *k1, yo, k1, ssk, k1, k2tog, k1, yo; rep from * 3 sts before marker, k2, yo, k1] four times. 8 sts increased

Round 12: [Knit to marker, slip marker] four times.

Round 13: [Yo, k2, *k1, yo, k2, sk2p, k2, yo; rep from * to 4 sts before marker, k3, yo, k1] four times. 8 sts increased

Round 14: [Knit to marker, slip marker] four times.

Round 15: [Yo, k3, *k1, yo, k1, k2tog, k1, ssk, k1, yo; rep from * to 5 sts before marker, k4, yo, k1] four times. 8 sts increased

Round 16: [Knit to marker, slip marker] four times.

Rep Rounds 9 to 16 once more, then rep Rounds 9 to 14 only once more. 128 sts

For garter stitch edging, work 3 rounds as follows, otherwise skip to bind (cast) off:

Next Round: Purl to end.

Next Round: Knit to end.

Next Round: Purl to end.

Bind (cast) off using a stretchy method as follows: k2, *slip both sts back to LH needle, k2tog tbl, k1; rep from * to end.

Fasten off, pulling yarn through last st.

Weave in ends and block to finished size.

SPARKLE

DESIGNER: CARMEN JORISSEN

YARN

A - Light Teal (Marseille 019)

B - Dark Teal (Multan 017)

NEEDLES

US size 2.5 (3mm) needles, or as needed to achieve gauge (tension)

GAUGE (TENSION)

31 sts x 30 rows = 4 x 4in (10 x 10cm) square

FINISHED SIZE

5¾ x 5¾in (14.5 x 14.5cm)

NOTES

This tile is worked in stockinette (stocking) stitch following the colourwork chart. The colour not in use should be stranded loosely across the back of the colour being used (see Techniques: Stranded Colourwork).

To make your colourwork look neat, wrap yarn B at the start of every row, preferably on the second stitch, as follows:

On RS rows, insert RH needle into next stitch (to be worked in yarn A), lay yarn B horizontally from right to left over RH needle, knit the stitch using yarn A. Yarn B is now wrapped. Make sure yarn B is not being pulled through the stitch.

On WS rows, insert RH needle into next stitch (to be worked in yarn A), hold yarn B up so that it lays vertically across RH needle, purl the stitch using yarn A.

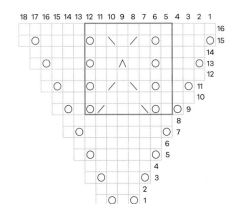

KEY

	knit
O	yo
/	k2tog
\	ssk
Λ	sk2p
	repeat

PATTERN

Using yarn A, cast on 44 sts.

Set-Up Row (WS): Using yarn A, purl to end.

Join in yarn B.

Work Rows 1 to 41 of chart.

Cut yarn B.

Next Row (WS): Using yarn A, purl to end.

Bind (cast) off all sts using yarn A.

Weave in ends and block to finished size.

KEY

 RS: knit
WS: purl

A

 B

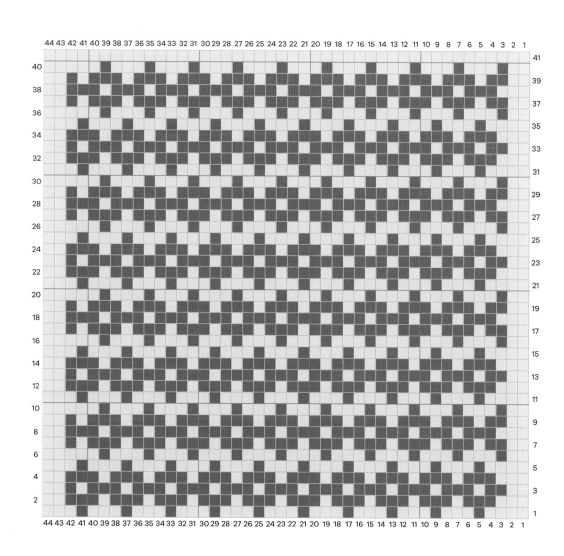

TERRACOTTA

DESIGNER: ANNAPLEXIS

YARN

A - Orange (Liverpool 065)

B - Cream (Toulouse 030)

C - Yellow (Dhaka 040)

D - Wine Red (Rabat 041)

NEEDLES

US size 1.5 (2.5mm) DPNs, or as needed to achieve gauge (tension)

ACCESSORIES

4 stitch markers, including one distinct for BOR

GAUGE (TENSION)

29 sts x 45 rounds = 4 x 4in (10 x 10cm) square

FINISHED SIZE

6¼ x 6¼in (16 x 16cm)

NOTES

This tile is worked in the round from the outer edge to the centre, working from the chart and including a garter stitch border.

When working the chart, the colour not in use should be stranded loosely across the back of the colour being used (see Techniques: Stranded Colourwork).

PATTERN

Using yarn A, cast on 180 sts. Join to work in the round, being careful not to twist the sts.

Round 1: [Work Row 1 of chart, place marker] four times, with final marker for BOR.

Continue working as set, slipping markers and working decreases as shown, and joining and cutting yarns as needed, until chart is complete. 12 sts

Cut all yarn strands and thread tail of yarn D through remaining sts, pulling tight to close the hole.

Weave in ends and block to finished size.

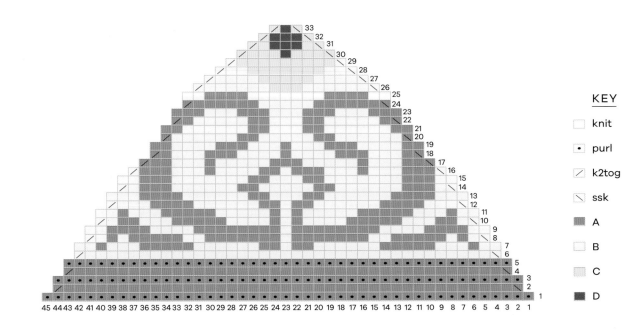

KEY

☐	knit
•	purl
◿	k2tog
◺	ssk
■	A
☐	B
▨	C
■	D

MIX IT

DESIGNER: ANNI HOWARD

YARN

A - Orange (Quebec 077)

B - Cream (Lyon 078)

C - Blue (Lahore 014)

NEEDLES

US size 3 (3.25mm) needles, or as
needed to achieve gauge (tension)

GAUGE (TENSION)

34 sts x 64 rows = 4 x 4in (10 x 10cm) square

FINISHED SIZE

6 x 6in (15 x 15cm)

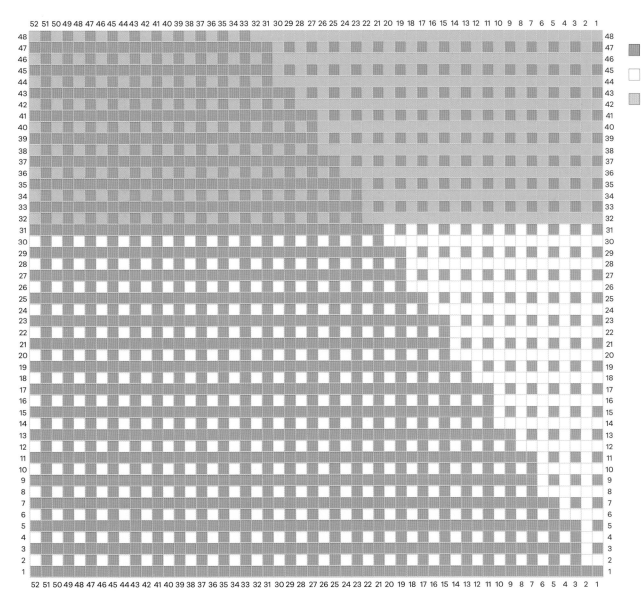

KEY

- ■ A
- □ B
- ▨ C

NOTES

Work this tile using mosaic knitting (see Techniques: Mosaic Knitting). Each chart row represents one RS row and one WS row. Knit sts that are the colour of the first st of the row, and slip the other colour.

PATTERN

Using yarn A, cast on 52 sts.

Work from chart as follows:

Row 1 (RS): Using yarn A, knit to end.

Row 1 (WS): Using yarn A, knit to end.

Row 2 (RS): Using yarn B, k2, *slip 1 purlwise, k1; rep from * to end.

Row 2 (WS): Using yarn B, *k1, move yarn to front, slip 1 purlwise, move yarn to back; rep from * to last 2 sts, k2.

Continue working from chart until Row 48 WS has been completed, cutting yarn B and joining yarn C after Row 31.

Bind (cast) off all sts knitwise using yarn C.

Weave in ends and block to finished size.

CRISS CROSS

DESIGNER: LYNNE ROWE

YARN

A - Orange (Leeds 046)

B - Pale Peach (Sydney 048)

NEEDLES

US size 2.5 (3mm) needles, or as needed to achieve gauge (tension)

GAUGE (TENSION)

34 sts x 34 rows = 4 x 4in (10 x 10cm) square

FINISHED SIZE

6¼ x 6¼in (16 x 16cm)

NOTES

This tile is worked in stockinette (stocking) stitch following the colourwork chart. The colour not in use should be stranded loosely across the back of the colour being used (see Techniques: Stranded Colourwork). A border is picked up and worked along each side in turn.

PATTERN

Using yarn A, cast on 49 sts.

Join in yarn B.

Work Rows 1 to 49 of chart.

Cut yarn B.

Bind (cast) off all sts purlwise using yarn A.

BORDER

Using yarn A, pick up and knit 47 sts along cast-on edge (note this is 2 sts less than original to accommodate for the change in tension).

Knit one row.

Bind (cast) off knitwise, leaving last st on needle.

**Rotate square to work along next side. Pick up and knit 1 st along edge of border just worked and then pick up and knit 47 sts evenly along edge to next corner. 48 sts

Knit one row.

Bind (cast) off knitwise, leaving last st on needle.

Rep from ** twice more to work remaining sides, making sure to pick up final st of last side in corner of the first border (you may want to pick up an extra st on final side).

Fasten off, pulling yarn through last st.

Weave in ends and block to finished size.

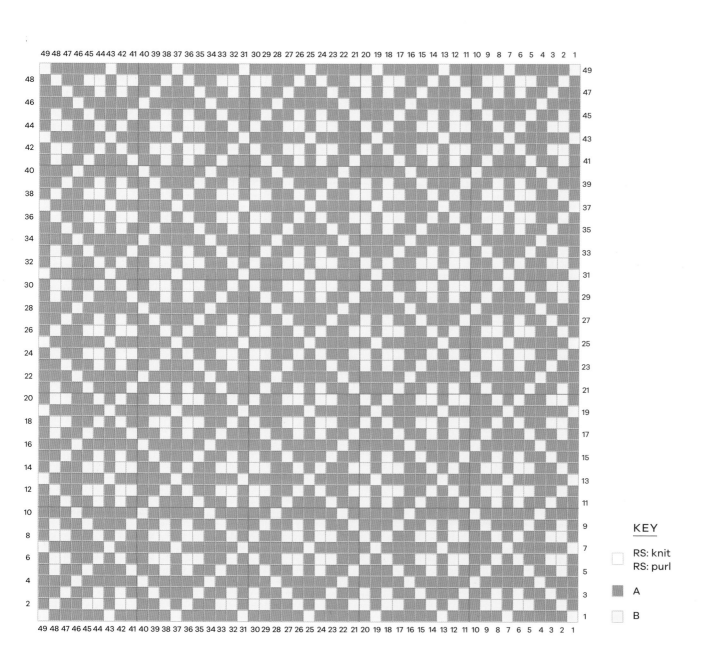

KEY

	RS: knit RS: purl
▨	A
▢	B

SMOCKED

DESIGNER: JACQUI GOULBOURN

YARN

Grey (Warsaw 072)

NEEDLES

US size 2 (2.75mm) needles, or as needed to achieve gauge (tension)

ACCESSORIES

Cable needle

GAUGE (TENSION)

30 sts x 40 rows = 4 x 4in (10 x 10cm) square

FINISHED SIZE

6 x 6in (15 x 15cm)

NOTES

The wrap3 stitch adds texture to the knitted tile. Be sure not to pull the wrap too tightly to avoid puckering the fabric.

Rows 3 to 10 are also shown in the chart.

Cables (see Special Abbreviations) are worked in the same way whether they are worked on RS or WS rows.

PATTERN

Cast on 45 sts.

Row 1 (RS): Knit.

Row 2: P1, k43, p1.

Row 3: K1, p1, k4, yo, [cdd, yo, k2, wrap3, k2, yo] three times, cdd, yo, k4, p1, k1.

Row 4: P1, k2, 1/1 RPC, p3, [p2, 1/1 LPC, k1, 1/1 RPC, p3] three times, p2, 1/1 LPC, k2, p1.

Row 5: K1, p3, 1/1 LPC, k1, [k2, 1/1 RPC, p3, 1/1 LPC, k1] 3 times, k2, 1/1 RPC, p3, k1.

Row 6: P1, k4, 1/1 RPC, p1, [1/1 LPC, k5, 1/1 RPC, p1] 3 times, 1/1 LPC, k4, p1.

Row 7: K1, p1, k4, [wrap3, k2, yo, cdd, yo, k2] 3 times, wrap3, k4, p1, k1.

Row 8: P1, k1, p3, 1/1 LPC, k1, [1/1 RPC, p5, 1/1 LPC, k1] 3 times, 1/1 RPC, p3, k1, p1.

Row 9: K1, p1, k2, 1/1 RPC, p1, [p2, 1/1 LPC, k3, 1/1 RPC, p1] 3 times, p2, 1/1 LPC, k2, p1, k1.

Row 10: P1, k1, p1, 1/1 LPC, k3, [k2, 1/1 RPC, p1, 1/1 LPC, k3] 3 times, k2, 1/1 RPC, p1, k1, p1.

Row 11 to 59: Rep Rows 3 to 10 seven times.

Row 60: K1, p43, k1.

Row 61: Purl.

Bind (cast) off all sts knitwise.

Weave in ends and block to finished size.

SPECIAL ABBREVIATIONS

1/1 LPC: 1 over 1 left cross with purl – slip 1 st to cable needle, hold at front of work, p1 from LH needle, k1 from cable needle

1/1 RPC: 1 over 1 right cross with purl – slip 1 st to cable needle, hold at back of work, k1 from LH needle, p1 from cable needle

wrap3: wrap 3 sts – k3, [bring yarn to front of work, slip these 3 sts from RH to LH needle, bring yarn to back of work, slip these 3 sts from LH to RH needle] twice

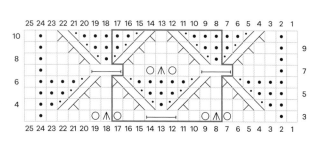

KEY

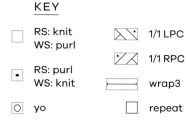

	RS: knit / WS: purl
	RS: purl / WS: knit
O	yo
⋀	cdd
	1/1 LPC
	1/1 RPC
	wrap3
	repeat

AFFINITY

DESIGNER: ARELLA SEATON

YARN

A - Light Blue (Ulsan 015)

B - Black (Cairo 070)

NEEDLES

US size 2.5 (3mm) needles, or as
needed to achieve gauge (tension)

GAUGE (TENSION)

31 sts x 60 rows = 4 x 4in (10 x 10cm)
square

FINISHED SIZE

6 x 6in (15 x 15cm)

KEY

□ A

■ B

NOTES

Work this tile using mosaic knitting (see Techniques: Mosaic Knitting). Each chart row represents one RS row and one WS row. Knit stitches that are the colour of the first stitch of the row, and slip the other colour.

PATTERN

Using yarn A, cast on 47 sts.

Work from chart as follows:

Row 1 (RS): Using yarn A, knit to end.

Row 1 (WS): Using yarn A, knit to end.

Row 2 (RS): Using yarn B, k1, slip 1 purlwise, k5, [slip 1 purlwise, k1] five times, slip 1 purlwise, k3, [slip 1 purlwise, k1] twice, slip 1 purlwise, k3, [slip 1 purlwise, k1] five times, slip 1 purlwise, k5, slip 1 purlwise, k1.

Row 2 (WS): Using yarn B, k1, move yarn to front, slip 1 purlwise, move yarn to back, k5, [move yarn to front, slip 1 purlwise, move yarn to back, k1] five times, move yarn to front, slip 1 purlwise, move yarn to back, k3, [move yarn to front, slip 1 purlwise, move yarn to back, k1] twice, move yarn to front, slip 1 purlwise, move yarn to back, k3, [move yarn to front, slip 1 purlwise, move yarn to back, k1] five times, move yarn to front, slip 1 purlwise, move yarn to back, k5, move yarn to front, slip 1 purlwise, move yarn to back, k1.

Continue working from chart until Row 45 WS has been completed.

Bind (cast) off all sts knitwise using yarn A.

Weave in ends and block to finished size.

BRICKLAYER

DESIGNER: HELEN BIRCH

YARN

A - Cream (Lyon 078)

B - Red (Naples 043)

NEEDLES

US size 2.5 (3mm) needles, or as needed to achieve gauge (tension)

GAUGE (TENSION)

29 sts x 52 rows = 4 x 4in (10 x 10cm) square

FINISHED SIZE

6 x 6in (15 x 15cm)

NOTES

Slip all stitches purlwise with the yarn held at the wrong side of the work (slipping with yarn in back on RS rows and with yarn in front on WS rows). The tile is finished with a border on each side.

PATTERN

Using yarn A, cast on 45 sts.

Knit 2 rows.

Join in yarn B.

Row 1 (RS): Using yarn B, k2, *slip 1, k3; rep from * to last 3 sts, slip 1, k2.

Row 2: Using yarn B, p2, *slip 1, p3; rep from * to last 3 sts, slip 1, p2.

Row 3: Using yarn A, knit to end.

Row 4: Using yarn A, knit to end.

Row 5: Using yarn B, k4, *slip 1, k3; rep from * to last 5 sts, slip 1, k4.

Row 6: Using yarn B, p4, *slip 1, p3; rep from * to last 5 sts, slip 1, p4.

Row 7: Using yarn A, knit to end.

Row 8: Using yarn A, knit to end.

Rep Rows 1 to 8 seven more times, then rep Rows 1 and 2 only once more.

Cut yarn B and continue with yarn A only.

Knit 3 rows.

Bind (cast) off all sts knitwise.

SIDE BORDERS (BOTH ALIKE)

With RS facing, and yarn A, starting at one corner pick up and knit 42 sts along row ends to next corner.

Bind (cast) off knitwise.

FINISHING

Weave in ends and block to finished size.

FIREWORKS

DESIGNER: ANNA NIKIPIROWICZ

YARN

A - Pink (Montreal 059)

B - Green (Canberra 031)

C - Blue (Lahore 014)

D - Beige (Buenos Aires 067)

NEEDLES

US size 4 (3.5mm) DPNs, or as needed to achieve gauge (tension)

ACCESSORIES

Stitch marker

US size G-6 (4mm) crochet hook for provisional cast on

Waste yarn in contrasting colour

GAUGE (TENSION)

21 sts x 38 rounds = 4 x 4in (10 x 10cm) square

FINISHED SIZE

6¼ x 6¼in (16 x 16cm)

NOTES

This tile is worked in the round from the centre to the outer edge, starting with a crochet provisional cast on (see Techniques: Crochet Provisional Cast On).

PATTERN

Using waste yarn and crochet hook, make 14 chains. Using yarn A and leaving a long tail, pick up and knit 12 sts in WS of crochet chain. Join to work in the round, being careful not to twist the sts. Mark the beginning of the round. 12 sts

Round 1: [K3, yo] four times.

Round 2: [M1L, k3, m1L, k1 tbl] four times. 24 sts

Round 3: Knit.

Change to yarn B.

Round 4: *M1L, [move yarn to front, slip 1 purlwise, move yarn to back, k1] twice, move yarn to front, slip 1 purlwise, move yarn to back m1L, k1 tbl; rep from * three more times. 32 sts

Round 5: Knit.

Round 6: [M1L, k8, m1L, k1 tbl] four times. 40 sts

Change to yarn C.

Round 7: *K1, [move yarn to front, slip 1 purlwise, move yarn to back, k1] four times, k1, k1 tbl; rep from * three more times.

Round 8: [M1L, k9, m1L, k1 tbl] four times. 48 sts

Round 9: Knit.

Change to yarn D.

Round 10: *M1L, [k1, move yarn to front, slip 1 purlwise, move yarn to back] five times, k1, m1L, k1 tbl; rep from * three more times.

Round 11: Knit.

Round 12: [M1L, k13, m1L, k1 tbl] four times. 64 sts

Change to yarn A.

Round 13: *K2, [move yarn to front, slip 1 purlwise, move yarn to back, k1] six times, k1, k1 tbl; rep from * three more times.

Round 14: [M1L, k15, m1L, k1 tbl] four times. 72 sts

Round 15: Knit.

Change to yarn B.

Round 16: *M1L, k2, [move yarn to front, slip 1 purlwise, move yarn to back, k1] seven times, k1, m1L, k1 tbl; rep from * three more times. 80 sts

Round 17: Knit.

Round 18: [M1L, k19, m1L, k1 tbl] four times. 88 sts

Change to yarn C.

Round 19: *K1, [move yarn to front, slip 1 purlwise, move yarn to back, k1] ten times, k1 tbl; rep from * three more times.

Round 20: [M1L, k21, m1L, k1 tbl] four times. 96 sts

Round 21: Knit.

Change to yarn D.

Round 22: *M1L, k1, [move yarn to front, slip 1 purlwise, move yarn to back, k1] 11 times, m1L, k1 tbl; rep from * three more times. 104 sts

Round 23: Knit.

Round 24: [M1L, k25, m1L, k1 tbl] four times. 112 sts

Change to yarn A.

Round 25: *K2, [move yarn to front, slip 1 purlwise, move yarn to back, k1] 12 times, k1, k1 tbl.

Round 26: [M1L, k27, m1L, k1 tbl] four times. 120 sts

Round 27: Knit.

Change to yarn B.

Round 28: *M1L, k2, [move yarn to front, slip 1 purlwise, move yarn to back, k1] 13 times, k1, m1L, k1 tbl; rep from * three more times. 128 sts

Round 29: Knit.

Bind (cast) off all sts.

Thread the yarn A cast-on yarn tail onto a tapestry needle. Unpick the provisional cast-on sts, placing them onto the tapestry needle. When all sts are released, pull tight to close the hole at the centre. Weave in ends and block to finished size.

DOORSTOP

DESIGNER: ANNI HOWARD

YARN

A - Cream (Lyon 078)

B - Blue (Lahore 014)

NEEDLES

US size 3 (3.25mm) needles, or as needed to achieve gauge (tension)

GAUGE (TENSION)

34 sts x 64 rows = 4 x 4in (10 x 10cm) square

FINISHED SIZE

6 x 6in (15 x 15cm)

NOTES

Work this tile using mosaic knitting (see Techniques: Mosaic Knitting). Each chart row represents one RS row and one WS row. Knit stitches that are the colour of the first stitch of the row, and slip the other colour.

PATTERN

Using yarn A, cast on 52 sts.

Work from chart as follows:

Row 1 (RS): Using yarn A, knit to end.

Row 1 (WS): Using yarn A, knit to end.

Row 2 (RS): Using yarn B, *k1, slip 1 purlwise, k1; rep from * to last 4 sts, k4.

Row 2 (WS): Using yarn B, k4, *move yarn to front, slip 1 purlwise, move yarn to back, k1; rep from * to end.

Continue working from chart until Row 48 WS has been completed.

Bind (cast) off all sts knitwise using yarn B.

Weave in ends and block to finished size.

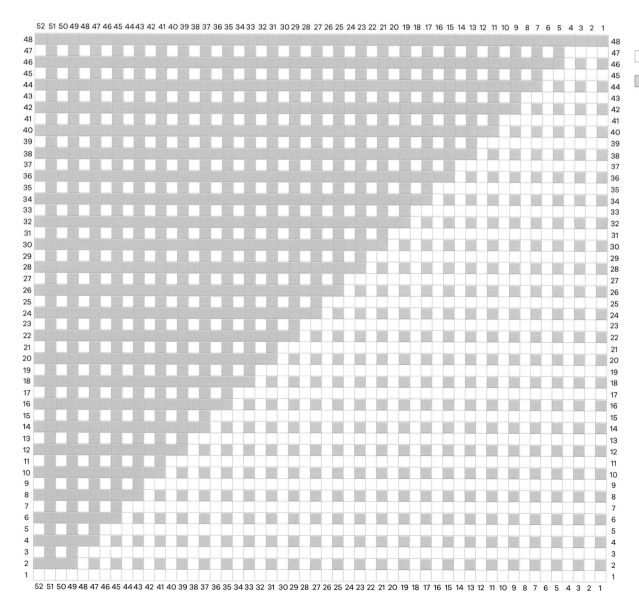

KEY

☐ A

▨ B

ARROWS

DESIGNER: LILY LANGMAN

YARN

A - Cream (Lyon 078)

B - Blue (Washington 013)

C - Teal Green (Pasay 022)

NEEDLES

US size 1.5 (2.5mm) needles, or as
needed to achieve gauge (tension)

GAUGE (TENSION)

29 sts x 45 rows = 4 x 4in (10 x 10cm) square

FINISHED SIZE

6¾ x 6in (17 x 15cm)

KEY

☐ RS: knit
WS: purl

☐ A

■ B

■ C

NOTES

This tile is knitted with a border of garter stitch on the top and bottom edges and 3 garter stitches on each side. The chart is worked in stockinette (stocking) stitch.

When working with two or three colours at once, the colours not in use should be stranded loosely across the back of the colour being used (see Techniques: Stranded Colourwork).

When stranding the yarn becomes difficult, use a separate ball of yarn for each colour and twist the yarn about to be used around the colour just used to link yarns together on WS to avoid a hole (see Techniques: Intarsia).

If you prefer to work a smaller tile without the border, cast on 43 sts using yarn D, work the chart, then bind (cast) off using yarn D.

PATTERN

Using yarn A, cast on 49 sts.

Work 4 rows of garter stitch.

Join in other colours as needed and work as follows:

Row 1 (RS): K3 using yarn A, knit Row 1 of chart, k3 using yarn A.

Row 2: K3 using yarn A, purl Row 2 of chart, k3 using yarn A.

Keeping first 3 sts and last 3 sts in garter stitch using yarn A throughout, continue until chart is complete.

Cut all colours except yarn A.

Work 3 rows of garter stitch.

Bind (cast) off all sts.

Weave in ends and block to finished size.

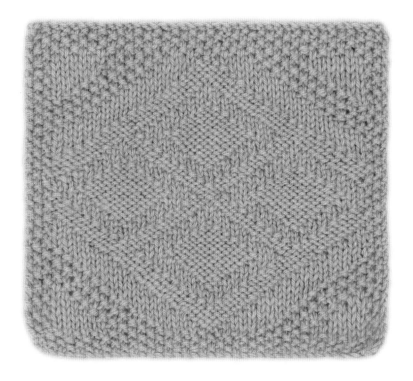

BROCADE

DESIGNER: ASHLEY GIBBONS

YARN

Light Green (Marseille 019)

NEEDLES

US size 2 (2.75mm) needles, or as needed to achieve gauge (tension)

GAUGE (TENSION)

30 sts x 40 rows = 4 x 4in (10 x 10cm) square

FINISHED SIZE

5¼ x 5¼in (13.5 x 13.5cm)

NOTES

This tile uses only knit and purl stitches to create a textured pattern.

PATTERN

Cast on 41 sts.

Row 1 (RS): *P1, k1; rep from * to last st, p1.

Rows 2 to 4: Rep Row 1 three times.

Row 5: P1, k1, p1, k7, [p1, k1] twice, [p1, k5] twice, [p1, k1] twice, p1, k7, p1, k1, p1.

Row 6: P1, k1, p7, [k1, p1] twice, k1, p5, k3, p5, [k1, p1] twice, k1, p7, k1, p1.

Row 7: P1, k1, p1, k5, [p1, k1] twice, p1, k5, p5, k5, [p1, k1] twice, p1, k5, p1, k1, p1.

Row 8: P1, k1, p5, [k1, p1] twice, k1, p5, k7, p5, [k1, p1] twice, k1, p5, k1, p1.

Row 9: P1, k1, p1, k3, p1, [k1, p1] twice, k5, p4, k1, p4, k5, [p1, k1] twice, p1, k3, p1, k1, p1.

Row 10: P1, k1, p3, [k1, p1] twice, k1, p5, k4, p3, k4, p5, [k1, p1] twice, k1, p3, k1, p1.

Row 11: [P1, k1] four times, p1, k5, p4, k5, p4, k5, [p1, k1] four times, p1.

Row 12: [P1, k1] four times, p5, k4, p3, k1, p3, k4, p5, [k1, p1] four times.

Row 13: [P1, k1] three times, p1, k5, p4, k3, p3, k3, p4, k5, [p1, k1] three times, p1.

Row 14: [P1, k1] three times, p5, k4, p3, k5, p3, k4, p5, [k1, p1] three times.

Row 15: [P1, k1] twice, p1, k5, p4, k3, p7, k3, p4, k5, [p1, k1] twice, p1.

Row 16: [P1, k1] twice, p5, k4, p3, k9, p3, k4, p5, [k1, p1] twice.

Row 17: P1, k1, p1, k5, p4, k3, p11, k3, p4, k5, p1, k1, p1.

Row 18: P1, k1, p5, k6, p3, k9, p3, k6, p5, k1, p1.

Row 19: P1, k1, p1, k3, p4, k1, p3, k3, p7, k3, p3, k1, p4, k3, p1, k1, p1.

Row 20: P1, k1, p3, k4, p3, k3, p3, k5, p3, k3, p3, k4, p3, k1, p1.

Row 21: [P1, k1] twice, p4, k5, [p3, k3] twice, p3, k5, p4, [k1, p1] twice.

Row 22.: P1, k1, p1, k4, p3, [k1, p3, k3, p3] twice, k1, p3, k4, p1, k1, p1.

Row 23: P1, k1, p4, [k3, p3] twice, k5, [p3, k3] twice, p4, k1, p1.

Row 24: P1, k1, p1, k2, p3, k5, [p3, k3] twice, p3, k5, p3, k2, p1, k1, p1.

Row 25: P1, k1, p2, k3, p7, k3, p3, k1, p3, k3, p7, k3, p2, k1, p1.

Row 26: P1, k1, p4, k9, p3, k5, p3, k9, p4, k1, p1.

Row 27: P1, k1, p1, k2, p11, k3, p3, k3, p11, k2, p1, k1, p1.

Row 28: Rep Row 26.

Row 29: Rep Row 25.

Row 30: Rep Row 24.

Row 31: Rep Row 23.

Row 32: Rep Row 22.

Row 33: Rep Row 21.

Row 34: Rep Row 20.

Row 35: Rep Row 19.

Row 36: Rep Row 18.

Row 37: Rep Row 17.

Row 38: Rep Row 16.

Row 39: Rep Row 15.

Row 40: Rep Row 14.

Row 41: Rep Row 13.

Row 42: Rep Row 12.

Row 43: Rep Row 11.

Row 44: Rep Row 10.

Row 45: Rep Row 9.

Row 46: Rep Row 8.

Row 47: Rep Row 7.

Row 48: Rep Row 6.

Row 49: Rep Row 5.

Rows 50 to 53: Rep Rows 1 to 4.

Bind (cast) off all sts as follows: *bind (cast) off 1 st purlwise, bind (cast) off 1 st knitwise; rep from * to last st, bind (cast) off purlwise.

Fasten off, pulling yarn through last st.

Weave in ends and block to finished size.

MODERN GEOMETRY

DESIGNER: SUZY RAI

YARN

A - Orange (Leeds 046)

B - Yellow (Brasov 038)

NEEDLES

US size 2.5 (3mm) needles, or as needed to achieve gauge (tension)

GAUGE (TENSION)

30 sts x 40 rows = 4 x 4in (10 x 10cm) square

FINISHED SIZE

5½ x 5½in (14 x 14cm)

NOTES

The chart is worked in stockinette (stocking) stitch throughout. Use a separate small ball of yarn for each colour and twist the yarns to avoid a hole (see Techniques: Intarsia).

PATTERN

Using yarn A, cast on 42 sts.

Join in yarn B as needed.

Work Rows 1 to 58 of chart.

Bind (cast) off all sts using yarn B.

Weave in ends and block to finished size.

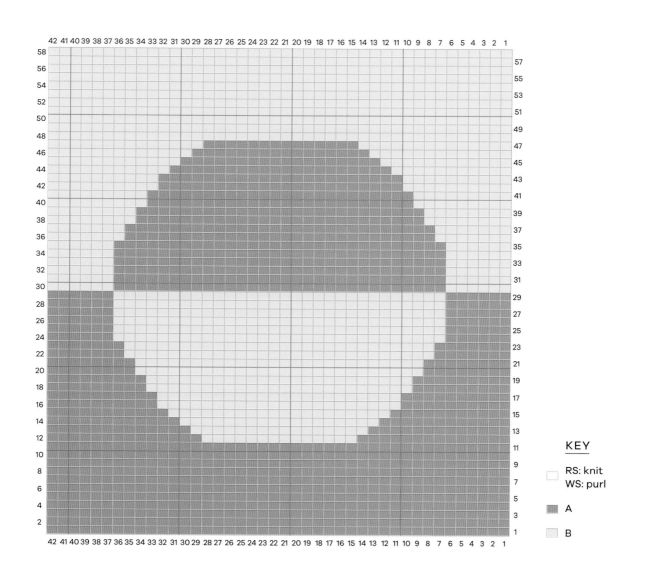

KEY

☐ RS: knit
WS: purl

■ A

■ B

OSTINATO

DESIGNER: ANNIKEN ALLIS

YARN

Indigo Blue (Dallas 003)

NEEDLES

US size 4 (3.5mm) DPNs, or as needed to achieve gauge (tension)

ACCESSORIES

4 stitch markers, including one distinct for BOR

GAUGE (TENSION)

20 sts x 37.5 rounds = 4 x 4in (10 x 10cm) square

FINISHED SIZE

Without garter stitch edging:
6¼ x 6¼in (16 x 16cm)

With garter stitch edging:
7 x 7in (18 x 18cm)

NOTES

This tile is worked in the round from the centre out. Yarn overs are worked before and after the corners on odd-numbered rounds for shaping.

Rounds 1 to 16 are also shown in the chart and are worked four times in each round. Work an additional 8-stitch repeat in each subsequent repeat of Rounds 9 to 16.

The garter stitch edging is optional.

PATTERN

Cast on 8 sts. Join to work in the round being careful not to twist stitches. Mark the beginning of the round.

Next Round: Knit.

Round 1: *[Yo, k1] twice, place marker; rep from * three more times, with final marker for BOR. 16 sts

Round 2: [Knit to marker, slip marker] four times.

Round 3: [Yo, k3, yo, k1] four times. 24 sts

Round 4: [Knit to marker, slip marker] four times.

Round 5: [Yo, k5, yo, k1] four times. 32 sts

Round 6: [Knit to marker, slip marker] four times.

Round 7: [Yo, k7, yo, k1] four times. 40 sts

Round 8: [Knit to marker, slip marker] four times.

Round 9: [Yo, *k2, yo, ssk, k1, k2tog, yo; rep from * to 2 sts before marker, k1, yo, k1, slip marker] four times. 8 sts increased

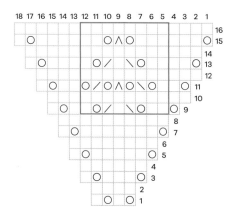

KEY

☐	knit
○	yo
╲	ssk
╱	k2tog
∧	sk2p
☐	repeat

Round 10: [Knit to marker, slip marker] four times.

Round 11: [Yo, k1, *k1, yo, ssk, yo, sk2p, yo, k2tog, yo; rep from * 3 sts before marker, k2, yo, k1] four times. 8 sts increased

Round 12: [Knit to marker, slip marker] four times.

Round 13: [Yo, k2, *k2, yo, ssk, k1, k2tog, yo, k1; rep from * to 4 sts before marker, k3, yo, k1] four times. 8 sts increased

Round 14: [Knit to marker, slip marker] four times.

Round 15: [Yo, k3, *k3, yo, sk2p, yo, k2; rep from * to 5 sts before marker, k4, yo, k1] four times. 8 sts increased

Round 16: [Knit to marker, slip marker] four times.

Rep Rounds 9 to 16 twice more. 136 sts

For garter stitch edging, work 3 rounds as follows, otherwise skip to bind (cast) off:

Next Round: Purl to end.

Next Round: Knit to end.

Next Round: Purl to end.

Bind (cast) off using a stretchy method as follows: k2, *slip both sts back to LH needle, k2tog tbl, k1; rep from * to end.

Fasten off, pulling yarn through last st.

Weave in ends and block to finished size.

BOBBLE DIAMOND

DESIGNER: LYNNE ROWE

YARN

Pale Lavender (Taipei 006)

NEEDLES

US size 2.5 (3mm) needles, or as needed to achieve gauge (tension)

GAUGE (TENSION)

30 sts x 42 rows = 4 x 4in (10 x 10cm) square

FINISHED SIZE

6 x 6in (15 x 15cm)

NOTES

This textured tile uses small bobbles to create the motif on a stockinette (stocking) stitch background.

Make bobble as follows: Knit into front and back of next stitch (2 stitches), turn, p2, turn, k2 then lift second stitch on RH needle over first stitch to bind (cast) off. Pull yarn tightly before knitting the next stitch and push bobble to the front of the work if needed.

PATTERN

Cast on 45 sts.

Row 1 (RS): Knit.

Row 2: Purl.

Rows 3 to 10: Rep Rows 1 and 2 four times.

Row 11: K12, [make bobble, k9] twice, make bobble, k12.

Row 12 and following WS rows: Purl.

Row 13: K13, make bobble, k7, make bobble, k1, make bobble, k7, make bobble, k13.

Row 15: K14, make bobble, k5, make bobble, k3, make bobble, k5, make bobble, k14.

Row 17: K15, make bobble, k3, make bobble, k5, make bobble, k3, make bobble, k15.

Row 19: K16, make bobble, k1, make bobble, k7, make bobble, k1, make bobble, k16.

Row 21: K17, make bobble, k9, make bobble, k17.

Row 23: Rep Row 19.

Row 25: Rep Row 17.

Row 27: Rep Row 15.

Row 29: Rep Row 13.

Row 31: Rep Row 11.

Row 33: Rep Row 13.

Row 35: Rep Row 15.

Row 37: Rep Row 17.

Row 39: Rep Row 19.

Row 41: Rep Row 21.

Row 43: Rep Row 19.

Row 45: Rep Row 17.

Row 47: Rep Row 15.

Row 49: Rep Row 13.

Row 51: Rep Row 11.

Row 52 (WS): Purl.

Row 53: Knit.

Rows 54 to 61: Rep Rows 52 and 53 four times.

Bind (cast) off all sts purlwise.

Weave in ends and block to finished size.

QUASAR

DESIGNER: SYLVIA WATTS-CHERRY

YARN

A - Medium Orange (Sevilla 076)

B - Dark Blue (Washington 013)

C - Light Blue (Lahore 014)

NEEDLES

US size 1.5 (2.5mm) needles, or as needed to achieve gauge (tension)

GAUGE (TENSION)

28 sts x 56 rows = 4 x 4in (10 x 10cm) square

FINISHED SIZE

6 x 6in (15 x 15cm)

NOTES

This tile is worked in garter stitch using intarsia (see Techniques: Intarsia), with each block of colour knit from a separate ball or bobbin of yarn. Twist the yarn about to be used around the colour just used to link yarns together on WS to avoid a hole.

PATTERN

Using cable cast-on method (see Techniques: Cable Cast On) and yarn B, cast on 42 sts.

Work Rows 1 to 82 of chart, joining in and changing colours as indicated.

Bind (cast) off all sts knitwise using yarn B.

Weave in ends, closing any gaps with yarn tails at colour changes, and block to finished size.

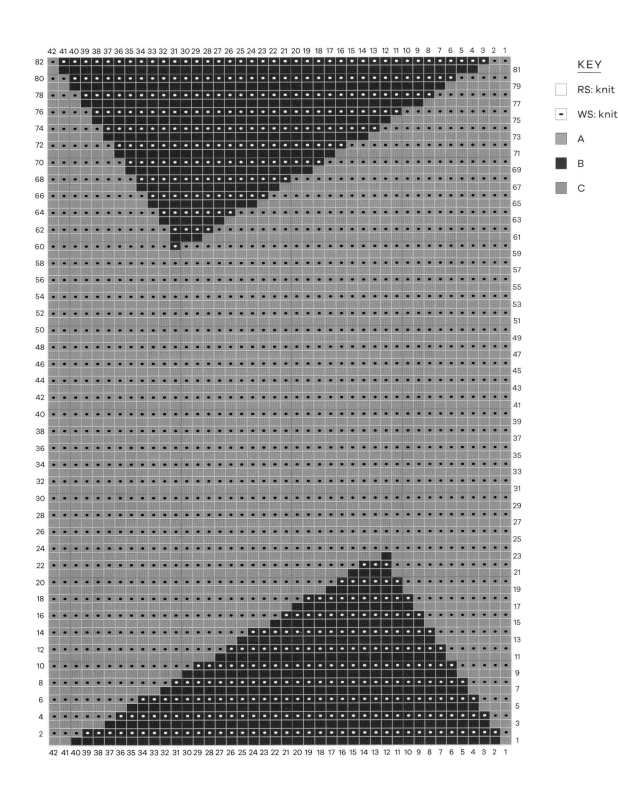

KEY

☐	RS: knit
⊡	WS: knit
▨	A
■	B
▨	C

A GLIMPSE OF THE MOON

....

DESIGNER: JOANNE FOWLER

YARN

A - Light Grey (Cota 024)

B - Dark Blue (Glasgow 002)

NEEDLES

US size 1.5 (2.5mm) needles, or as needed to achieve gauge (tension)

ACCESSORIES

4 locking stitch markers (A-D)

GAUGE (TENSION)

28 sts x 52 rows = 4 x 4in (10 x 10cm) square

FINISHED SIZE

6 x 6in (15 x 15cm)

NOTES

The tile is knitted diagonally from one corner to another. The rounded motif is created with the increases in garter stitch followed by the sharp decreases to finish shaping the square.

If you find it fiddly to work the lifted increases in Row 1 as you are lifting from the cast-on row, you can substitute a twisted yarn over or backwards loop (e-loop) increase on this row instead, as long as it does not leave a hole. When not mentioned, slip stitch markers as you come to them.

It is recommended to use locking stitch markers so you can easily move markers C and D as instructed.

Make sure to stretch the quarter circle into a rounder shape when blocking.

SPECIAL ABBREVIATIONS

Rli: right lifted increase – lift the RH leg of st below next st on LH needle onto LH needle and knit it

Lli: left lifted increase – lift the LH leg of st 2 rows below st on RH needle onto LH needle and knit it through the back loop

PATTERN

Using long tail cast-on method (see Techniques: Long Tail/Continental Cast On) and yarn A, cast on 3 sts.

INCREASE SECTION

Row 1 (RS): K1, Lli, Rli, k1, place marker A, Lli, Rli, K1. 7 sts

Row 2: P1, knit to marker A, slip marker, p1, knit to last st, p1.

Row 3: Knit.

Row 4: P1, knit to marker A, slip marker, p1, place marker B, knit to last st, p1.

Row 5: K1, Lli, knit to marker B, Rli, slip marker, k1, Lli, knit to last st, Rli, k1. 4 sts increased

Row 6: P1, knit to marker A, slip marker, p1, knit to last st, p1.

Row 7: Knit.

Row 8: P1, knit to marker A, slip marker, p1, knit to last st, p1.

Rows 9 to 40: Rep Rows 5 to 8 eight times. 43 sts

Cut yarn A and join in yarn B.

Rows 41 to 64: Using yarn B, rep Rows 5 to 8 six times. 67 sts

DECREASE SECTION

Markers C and D are placed to indicate the end of the working row. Leave unworked sts to the 'outside' of these markers until instructed.

Row 65: Bind (cast) off 5 sts, knit to marker B, Rli, slip marker, k1, slip marker, Lli, knit to last 5 sts, place marker C, turn. 64 sts

Row 66: Knit to marker A, slip marker, p1, knit to last 5 sts, place marker D, turn.

Row 67: Knit to 5 sts before marker C, place new marker C at this point.

Row 68: Knit to marker A, slip marker, p1, knit to 4 sts before marker D, place new marker D at this point.

Row 69: Knit to marker B, Rli, slip marker, k1, slip marker, Lli, knit to 4 sts before marker C, place new marker C at this point. 66 sts

Row 70: Rep Row 68.

Row 71: Knit to 4 sts before marker C, place new marker C at this point.

Row 72: Knit to marker A, slip marker, p1, knit to 3 sts before marker D, place new marker D at this point.

Row 73: Knit to marker B, Rli, slip marker, k1, slip marker, Lli, knit to 3 sts before marker C, place new marker C at this point. 2 sts increased

Row 74: Rep Row 72.

Row 75: Knit to 3 sts before marker C, place new marker C at this point.

Rows 76 to 79: Rep Rows 72 to 75. 70 sts

Rows 80 and 81: Rep Rows 72 and 73. 72 sts

Row 82: Knit to marker A, slip marker, p1, knit to 2 sts before marker D, place new marker D at this point.

Row 83: Knit to 2 sts before marker C, place new marker C at this point.

Row 84: Rep Row 82.

Row 85: Knit to marker B, Rli, slip marker, k1, slip marker, Lli, knit to 2 sts before marker C, place new marker C at this point. 74 sts

Row 86: Rep Row 82.

Row 87: K3tog (corner). 72 sts

Using attached yarn B and removing markers as you go, bind (cast) off sts to next corner. Cut yarn. With WS facing, rejoin yarn B at k3tog corner st. Removing markers as you go, bind (cast) off remaining sts to next corner.

Weave in ends and block to finished size, taking care not to stretch out the ribbed sections.

CULTIVATED

DESIGNER: ANNAPLEXIS

YARN

A - Green (Abu Dhabi 032)

B - Aubergine (Ajman 049)

C - Pale Peach (Sydney 048)

D - Purple (Santiago 053)

E - Pale Yellow (Delhi 039)

F - Wine Red (Rabat 041)

NEEDLES

US size 1.5 (2.5mm) needles, or as needed to achieve gauge (tension)

GAUGE (TENSION)

29 sts x 45 rows = 4 x 4in (10 x 10cm) square

FINISHED SIZE

6¼ x 6¼in (16 x 16cm)

NOTES

This tile is knitted with a garter stitch border and a stockinette (stocking) stitch background, with lines of Latvian braids.

The braids are worked in two colours over three rows, and will twist the yarns and untwist them as you work.

Slip the first stitch of each row purlwise.

PATTERN

Using yarn A, cast on 45 sts.

Row 1 (WS): Slip 1, knit to end.

Rows 2 to 5: Rep Row 1 four more times.

Row 6 (RS): Slip 1, k3 using yarn A, stranding yarn not in use across back (WS) of work, join in yarn B, k1 using yarn B, [k1 using yarn A, k1 using yarn B] 18 times, k4 using yarn A.

Row 7 (WS): Slip 1, k3 using yarn A, stranding yarn not in use across back (RS) of work and picking up new colour from underneath other yarn every time and allowing yarn to twist, k1 using yarn B, [k1 using yarn A, k1 using yarn B] 18 times, bring yarn B to front of work, k4 using yarn A.

Do not untwist the yarns, they will untwist as you work Row 8.

Row 8 (RS): Slip 1, k3 using yarn A, stranding yarn not in use across front (RS) of work and picking up new colour from underneath other yarn every time and allowing yarn to untwist, p1 using yarn B, [p1 using yarn A, p1 using yarn B] 18 times, k4 using yarn A.

Cut yarn B.

Row 9 (WS): Using yarn A, slip 1, k3, p37, k4.

Row 10 (RS): Using yarn A, slip 1, knit to end.

Rows 11 to 19: Rep Rows 9 and 10 four times then Row 9 once more.

Rows 20 to 22: Rep Rows 6 to 8 using yarn C instead of yarn B.

Cut yarn C.

Rows 23 to 33: Rep Rows 9 to 19.

Rows 34 to 36: Rep Rows 6 to 8 using yarn D instead of yarn B.

Cut yarn D.

Rows 37 to 47: Rep Rows 9 to 19.

Rows 48 to 50: Rep Rows 6 to 8 using yarn E instead of yarn B.

Cut yarn E.

Rows 51 to 61: Rep Rows 9 to 19.

Rows 62 to 64: Rep Rows 6 to 8 using yarn F instead of yarn B.

Cut yarn F.

Row 65: Rep Row 9.

Row 66: Slip 1, knit to end.

Rows 67 to 71: Rep Row 66 five more times.

Bind (cast) off all sts.

Weave in ends and block to finished size.

FOUR CANDLES

DESIGNER: ARELLA SEATON

YARN

A - Cream (Lyon 078)

B - Black (Cairo 070)

NEEDLES

US size 2.5 (3mm) needles, or as needed to achieve gauge (tension)

GAUGE (TENSION)

31 sts x 60 rows = 4 x 4in (10 x 10cm) square

FINISHED SIZE

6 x 6in (15 x 15cm)

NOTES

Work this tile using mosaic knitting (see Techniques: Mosaic Knitting). Each chart row represents one RS row and one WS row. Knit stitches that are the colour of the first stitch of the row, and slip the other colour.

PATTERN

Using yarn A, cast on 47 sts.

Work from chart as follows:

Row 1 (RS): Using yarn A, knit to end.

Row 1 (WS): Using yarn A, knit to end.

Row 2 (RS): Using yarn B, [k1, slip 1 purlwise] nine times, k3, [slip 1 purlwise, k1] twice, slip 1 purlwise, k3, [slip 1 purlwise, k1] nine times.

Row 2 (WS): Using yarn B, [k1, move yarn to front, slip 1 purlwise, move yarn to back] nine times, k3, [move yarn to front, slip 1 purlwise, move yarn to back, k1] twice, move yarn to front, slip 1 purlwise, move yarn to back, k3, [move yarn to front, slip 1 purlwise, move yarn to back, k1] nine times.

Continue working from chart until Row 45 WS has been completed.

Bind (cast) off all sts knitwise using yarn A.

Weave in ends and block to finished size.

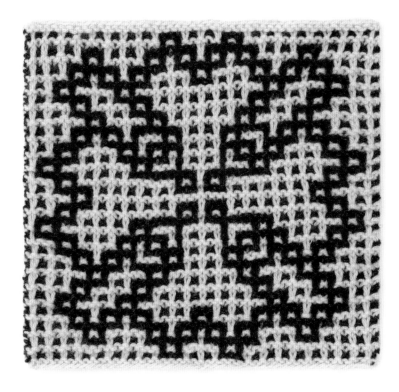

KEY

☐ A

■ B

HELIOS

DESIGNER: ANNAPLEXIS

YARN

A - Dark Orange (Mexico City 075)

B - Yellow (Dhaka 040)

NEEDLES

US size 1.5 (2.5mm) needles, or as needed to achieve gauge (tension)

GAUGE (TENSION)

29 sts x 45 rows = 4 x 4in (10 x 10cm) square

FINISHED SIZE

6¼ x 5½in (16 x 14cm)

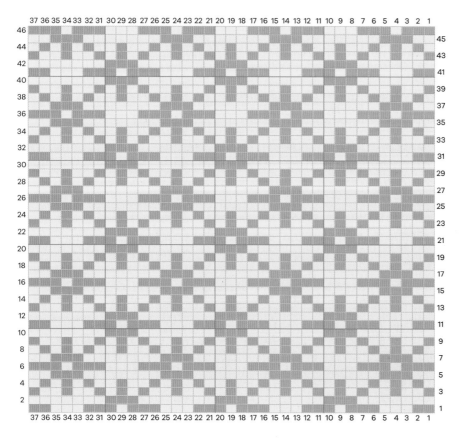

KEY

RS: knit
WS: purl

A

B

NOTES

This tile is knitted with a garter stitch border. The chart is worked in stockinette (stocking) stitch.

When working with two colours at once, the colours not in use should be stranded loosely across the back of the colour being used (see Techniques: Stranded Colourwork).

Slip the first st of each row purlwise.

PATTERN

Using yarn A, cast on 45 sts.

Next Row: Slip 1, knit to end.

Rep this row four more times.

Join in yarn B and work as follows:

Row 1 (RS): Slip 1, k3 using yarn A, knit Row 1 of chart, k4 using yarn A.

Row 2: Slip 1, k3 using yarn A, purl Row 2 of chart, k4 using yarn A.

Keeping first 4 sts and last 4 sts in garter stitch as set using yarn A throughout, continue until chart is complete.

Cut yarn B and continue with yarn A only.

Next Row: Using yarn A, slip 1, knit to end.

Rep this row five more times.

Bind (cast) off all sts.

Weave in ends and block to finished size.

GINGHAM

DESIGNER: CARMEN JORISSEN

YARN

A - Pale Lavender (Taipei 006)

B - Orange (Liverpool 065)

NEEDLES

US size 2.5 (3mm) needles, or as needed to achieve gauge (tension)

GAUGE (TENSION)

31 sts x 30 rows = 4 x 4in (10 x 10cm) square

FINISHED SIZE

5¾ x 5¾in (14.5 x 14.5cm)

NOTES

This tile is worked in stockinette (stocking) stitch following the colourwork chart. The colour not in use should be stranded loosely across the back of the colour being used (see Techniques: Stranded Colourwork).

To make your colourwork look neat, wrap yarn B at the start of every row, preferably on the second stitch, as follows:

On RS rows, insert RH needle into next stitch (to be worked in yarn A), lay yarn B horizontally from right to left over RH needle, knit the stitch using yarn A. Yarn B is now wrapped. Make sure yarn B is not being pulled through the stitch.

On WS rows, insert RH needle into next stitch (to be worked in yarn A), hold yarn B up so that it lays vertically across RH needle, purl the stitch using yarn A.

PATTERN

Using yarn A, cast on 44 sts.

Set-Up Row (WS): Using yarn A, purl to end.

Join in yarn B.

Work Rows 1 to 41 of chart.

Cut yarn B and continue with yarn A only.

Next Row (WS): Using yarn A, purl to end.

Bind (cast) off all sts.

Weave in ends and block to finished size.

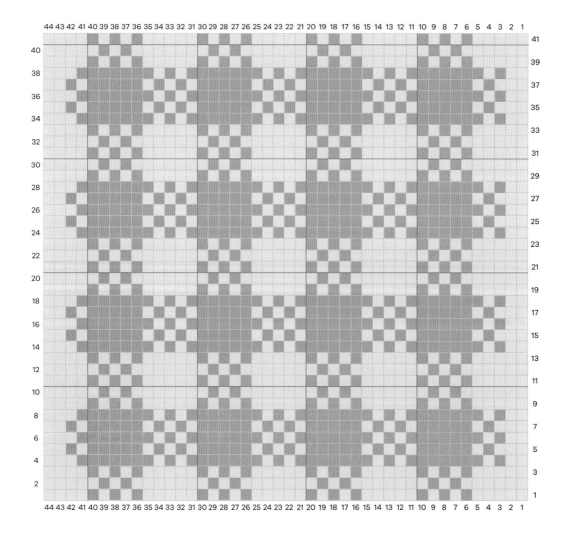

Key

RS: knit
WS: purl

A

B

TENDER LOVE

DESIGNER: LYNNE ROWE

YARN

A - Orange (Leeds 046)

B - Pale Peach (Sydney 048)

NEEDLES

US size 2.5 (3mm) needles, or as needed to achieve gauge (tension)

GAUGE (TENSION)

30 sts x 43 rows = 4 x 4in (10 x 10cm) square

FINISHED SIZE

6 x 6in (15 x 15cm)

NOTES

The heart motif is knitted using both yarn A and yarn B held together and worked as if they were one strand for the contrast colour (CC). Pick up and drop the yarn B strand as needed.

PATTERN

Using yarn A, cast on 43 sts.

Starting with a RS (knit) row, work 12 rows in stockinette (stocking) stitch.

Work from chart as follows:

Row 1 (RS): K20 using yarn A, join in yarn B and k3 CC using yarn A and yarn B held together, drop yarn B, k20 using yarn A.

Row 2 (WS): P20 using yarn A, pick up yarn B and p3 CC using yarn A and yarn B held together, drop yarn B, p20 using yarn A.

Continue working from chart until Row 34 has been completed.

Cut yarn B and continue with yarn A.

Starting with a RS (knit) row, work 12 rows in stockinette (stocking) stitch.

Bind (cast) off all sts.

Weave in ends and block to finished size.

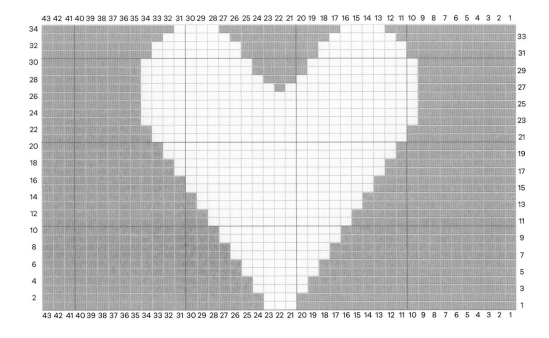

KEY

	RS: knit WS: purl
▨	A
☐	CC

AERATION

DESIGNER: ANNA NIKIPIROWICZ

YARN

Grey (Izmir 073)

NEEDLES

US size 4 (3.5mm) DPNs, or as needed to achieve gauge (tension)

ACCESSORIES

Stitch marker

US size G-6 (4mm) crochet hook for provisional cast on

Waste yarn in contrasting colour

GAUGE (TENSION)

18 sts x 34 rounds = 4 x 4in (10 x 10cm) square

FINISHED SIZE

6¼ x 6¼in (16 x 16cm)

NOTES

This tile is worked in the round from the centre to the outer edge, starting with a crochet provisional cast on (see Techniques: Crochet Provisional Cast On).

PATTERN

Using waste yarn and crochet hook, make 14 chains. Using working yarn and leaving a long tail, pick up and knit 12 sts in WS of crochet chain. Join to work in the round, being careful not to twist the sts. Mark the beginning of the round. 12 sts

Round 1: [K3, yo] four times. 16 sts

Round 2 and even-numbered rounds to Round 24: Knit.

Rnd 3: [Yo, k3, yo, k1 tbl] four times. 24 sts

Rnd 5: [Yo, k5, yo, k1 tbl] four times. 32 sts

Rnd 7: [Yo, k7, yo, k1 tbl] four times. 40 sts

Rnd 9: [Yo, k9, yo, k1 tbl] four times. 48 sts

Rnd 11: [Yo, k4, yo, sk2p, yo, k4 yo, k1 tbl] four times. 56 sts

Rnd 13: [Yo, k2, yo, sk2p, yo, k3, yo, sk2p, yo, k2, yo, k1 tbl] four times. 64 sts

Rnd 15: [Yo, k1, skpo, yo, k3, yo, sk2p, yo, k3, yo, skpo, k1, yo, k1 tbl] four times. 72 sts

Rnd 17: [Yo, k4, yo, sk2p, yo, k3, yo, sk2p, yo, k4, yo, k1 tbl] four times. 80 sts

Rnd 19: *Yo, k2, [yo, sk2p, yo, k3] twice, yo, sk2p, yo, k2, yo, k1 tbl; rep from * three more times. 88 sts

Rnd 21: *Yo, k1, skpo, yo, k3, [yo, sk2p, yo, k3] twice, yo, skpo, k1, yo, k1 tbl; rep from * three more times. 96 sts

Rnd 23: *Yo, k4, yo, sk2p, yo, [k3, yo, sk2p, yo] twice, k4, yo, k1 tbl; rep from * three more times. 104 sts

Rnd 25: *Yo, k2, [yo, sk2p, yo, k3] three times, yo, sk2p, yo, k2, yo, k1 tbl; rep from * three more times. 112 sts

Round 26: Knit.

Bind (cast) off all sts.

Thread cast-on yarn tail onto a tapestry needle. Unpick the provisional cast-on sts, placing them onto the tapestry needle. When all sts are released, pull tight to close the hole at the centre. Weave in ends and block to finished size.

PERSIAN SHIELD

DESIGNER: KAROLINA ADAMCZYK

YARN

A - Blue (Boston 011)

B - Pink (Bangalore 052)

NEEDLES

US size 1.5 (2.5mm) DPNs, or as needed to achieve gauge (tension)

ACCESSORIES

4 stitch markers, including one distinct for BOR

GAUGE (TENSION)

29 sts x 38 rounds = 4 x 4in (10 x 10cm) square

FINISHED SIZE

6½ x 6½in (16.5 x 16.5cm)

NOTES

This tile is worked in the round from the outer edge to the centre. It begins with a ribbed border, with markers indicating the corners of the square where decreases shape the work.

The chart is repeated four times in each round. When working the chart, the colour not in use should be stranded loosely across the back of the colour being used (see Techniques: Stranded Colourwork).

PATTERN

Using yarn A, cast on 180 sts. Join to work in the round, being careful not to twist the sts.

Round 1: *[K1, p1] 22 times, k1, place marker; rep from * three more times, with the final marker for BOR.

Round 2: *Ssk, [k1, p1] 20 times, k1, k2tog, slip marker; rep from * three more times. 172 sts

Round 3: *K1, [k1, p1] 20 times, k2, slip marker; rep from * three more times.

Round 4: *Ssk, knit to 2 sts before marker, k2tog, slip marker; rep from * three more times. 164 sts

Join in yarn B.

Repeating chart four times in each round, work Rows 1 to 25 of chart, decreasing before and after markers on rounds as indicated. 28 sts

Cut yarn B and continue with yarn A only.

Next Round: Knit.

Next Round: [K2tog] 14 times, removing all markers. 14 sts

Cut yarn A and thread end through remaining sts, pulling tight to close the hole.

Weave in ends and block to finished size.

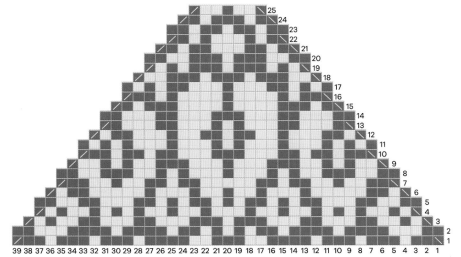

KEY

☐	knit
◲	ssk
◱	k2tog
■	A
▨	B

STARLIT SKY

DESIGNER: JOANNE FOWLER

YARN

A - Dark Blue (Glasgow 002)

B - Light Grey (Cota 024)

NEEDLES

US size 1.5 (2.5mm) needles, or as needed to achieve gauge (tension)

GAUGE (TENSION)

29 sts x 43 rows = 4 x 4in (10 x 10cm) square

FINISHED SIZE

6 x 6in (15 x 15cm)

NOTES

The tile features slipped stitch rows and eyelet rows in two colours to produce a colourful and textured fabric. Slip all stitches purlwise and with yarn held in back unless otherwise noted.

Work the knot-stitch as follows: Working into one stitch: pull a loop through knitwise, yo, pull a second loop through knitwise (resulting in three loops on RH needle), pull stitch off LH needle. Note: you may need to hold the yo in place until final loop is pulled through.

PATTERN

Using yarn A, cast on 43 sts.

Row 1 (WS): Using yarn A, purl.

Row 2: Using yarn A, knit.

Row 3: Using yarn A, purl.

Join in yarn B but do not cut yarn A.

Row 4: Using yarn B, slip 1, *knot-stitch, slip 1; rep from * to end.

Row 5: Using yarn B, slip 1, *k3tog, slip 1; rep from * to end.

Do not cut yarn B.

Row 6: Using yarn A, knit.

Row 7: Using yarn A, purl.

Rows 8 and 9: Catching yarn B along edge before first st to avoid a long float, rep Rows 6 and 7 using yarn A.

Row 10: Using yarn B, slip 2, *knot-stitch, slip 1; rep from * to last st, slip 1.

Row 11: Using yarn B, slip 1 with yarn held in front, slip 1, *k3tog tbl, slip 1; rep from * to last st, slip 1 with yarn held in front.

Do not cut yarn B.

Rows 12 to 21: Rep Rows 2 to 11.

Cut yarn B and continue with yarn A.

Rows 22 and 23: Rep Rows 2 and 3.

Rows 24 and 25: Knit.

Rows 26 and 27: Rep Rows 2 and 3.

Row 28: K1, *yo, k2tog; rep from * to end.

Row 29: Purl.

Row 30: K2, *yo, k2tog; rep from * to last st, k1.

Row 31: Purl.

Rows 32 to 39: Rep Rows 28 to 31 twice.

Rows 40 and 41: Knit.

Rows 42 and 43: Rep Rows 2 and 3.

Rows 44 to 63: Rep Rows 2 to 11 twice, joining in yarn B as needed.

Cut yarn B and continue with yarn A.

Row 64: Knit.

Row 65: Purl.

Bind (cast) off all sts.

Weave in ends and block to finished size.

SOLAR SYSTEM

DESIGNER: ARELLA SEATON

YARN

A - Cream (Lyon 078)

B - Light Blue (Ulsan 015)

C - Dark Blue (Bucharest 001)

D - Yellow (Brasov 038)

E - Black (Cairo 070)

NEEDLES

US size 2.5 (3mm) DPNs, or as
needed to achieve gauge (tension)

ACCESSORIES

4 stitch markers, including one distinct
for BOR

GAUGE (TENSION)

50 sts x 49 rounds = 4 x 4in (10 x 10cm)
square

FINISHED SIZE

8 x 8in (20 x 20cm)

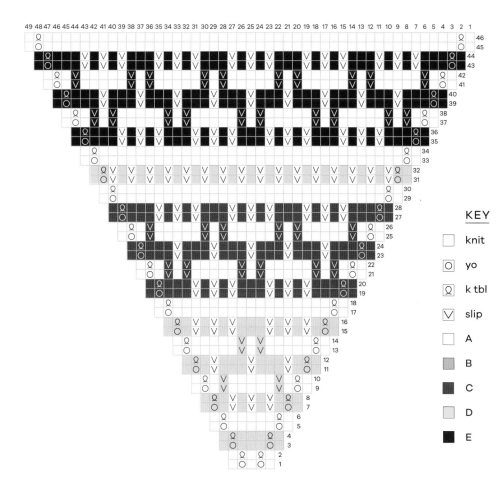

KEY

☐	knit
Ⓞ	yo
Ⓠ	k tbl
☑	slip
☐	A
▨	B
■	C
▢	D
■	E

NOTES

This tile is worked in the round from the centre to the outer edge, with only one colour worked in each round. Slip all stitches purlwise with yarn stranded loosely across the back of the work.

PATTERN

Using yarn A, cast on 12 sts using a centre-out cast-on method (see Techniques: Centre-Out Cast On) or cast on with your preferred method, leaving a long yarn tail. Join to work in the round, being careful not to twist the sts. Mark the beginning of the round. 12 sts

Set-Up Round: [K3, place marker] four times, with final marker for BOR.

Repeating chart four times in each round, work Rows 1 to 46 of chart, increasing before and after markers on odd-numbered rounds as indicated and joining in yarns as required. 196 sts

Cut all yarns except yarn A.

Bind (cast) off all sts.

Use the cast-on yarn tail to close the hole at the centre if needed. Weave in ends and block to finished size.

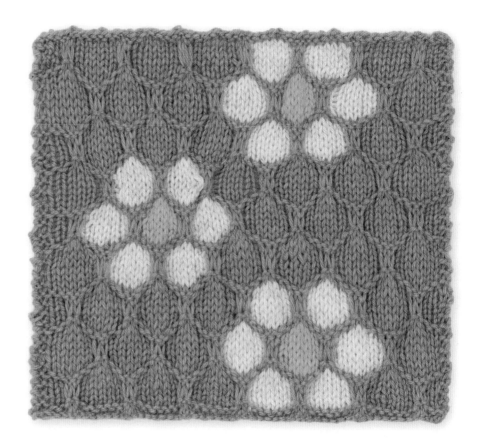

FIELD OF DAISIES

· · · · · · · · · ·

DESIGNER: DANIELLE HOLKE

YARN

A - Green (Abu Dhabi 032)

B - Light Grey (Cota 024)

C - Yellow (Tehran 036)

NEEDLES

US size 2 (2.75mm) needles, or as needed to achieve gauge (tension)

GAUGE (TENSION)

36 sts x 46 rows = 4 x 4in (10 x 10cm) square

FINISHED SIZE

6¼ x 6¼in (16 x 16cm)

NOTES

Slipped stitches create a textured hexagon pattern that seems to 'float' over the stockinette (stocking) stitch background. The tile is worked with a border in garter stitch, with stitches slipped at the start of rows to create a firm edge. Work slip stitches at the start of rows knitwise holding yarn in back.

For the pattern repeat, slip stitches purlwise, stranding the yarn along the WS of the work. When working a RS row hold yarn at the back of the work, and when working a WS row hold yarn at the front of the work. Make sure not to pull too tightly so that the fabric does not pucker.

The colourwork is worked in the intarsia technique (see Techniques: Intarsia).

PATTERN

Using yarn A, cast on 58 sts.

Row 1 (RS): Knit.

Row 2: Slip 1 knitwise, knit to end.

Join in other colours as needed and work as follows:

Row 3 (RS): Slip 1 knitwise, k1 using yarn A, work Row 3 of chart, k2 using yarn A.

Row 4: Slip 1 knitwise, k1 using yarn A, work Row 4 of chart, k2 using yarn A.

Keeping first 2 sts and last 2 sts in garter stitch using yarn A and slipping first st of each row, continue until chart is complete.

Cut yarn B and yarn C.

Rows 73 and 74: Using yarn A, slip 1 knitwise, knit to end.

Bind (cast) off all sts using yarn A.

Weave in ends and block to finished size.

KEY

☐ RS: knit
WS: purl

▪ WS: knit

∨ slip 1 purlwise

■ A

☐ B

☐ C

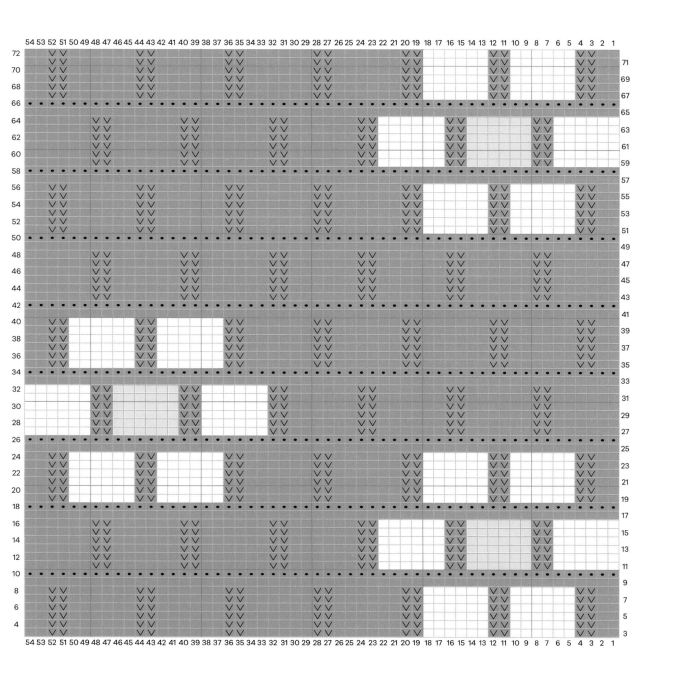

PARALLAX

DESIGNER: ANNAPLEXIS

YARN

A - Orange (Liverpool 065)

B - Cream (Toulouse 030)

NEEDLES

US size 1.5 (2.5mm) DPNs, or as needed to achieve gauge (tension)

ACCESSORIES

4 stitch markers, including one distinct for BOR

Cable needle

GAUGE (TENSION)

29 sts x 45 rounds = 4 x 4in (10 x 10cm) square

FINISHED SIZE

6¼ x 6¼in (16 x 16cm)

NOTES

This tile is worked in the round from the outer edge to the centre, working from the chart and including a garter stitch border.

When working the chart, the colour not in use should be stranded loosely across the back of the colour being used (see Techniques: Stranded Colourwork).

The twist stitches are worked in both colours (see Special Abbreviations).

PATTERN

Using yarn A, cast on 180 sts. Join to work in the round, being careful not to twist the sts.

Round 1: [Work Row 1 of chart, place marker] four times, with final marker for BOR.

Continue working as set, slipping markers and working decreases, twists and increases as shown, and joining in yarn B as needed, until chart is complete. 12 sts

Cut both yarn strands and thread tail of yarn A through remaining sts, pulling tight to close the hole.

Weave in ends and block to finished size.

SPECIAL ABBREVIATIONS

LT: left twist with two colours – slip next st onto cable needle, hold at front of work, k1 from LH needle with yarn B, k1 from cable needle with yarn A

RT: right twist with two colours – slip next st onto cable needle, hold at back of work, k1 from LH needle with yarn A, k1 from cable needle with yarn B

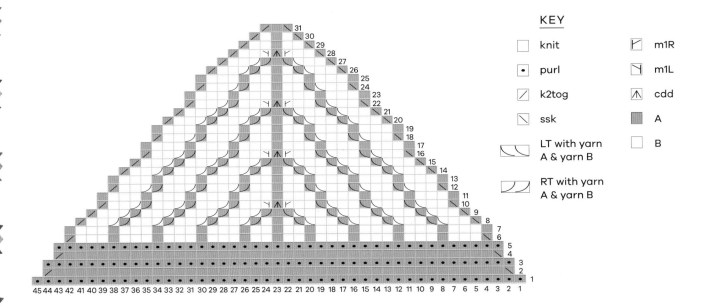

KEY

☐ knit	✎ m1R
• purl	✎ m1L
✎ k2tog	⋏ cdd
✎ ssk	▨ A
◝ LT with yarn A & yarn B	☐ B
◝ RT with yarn A & yarn B	

DOGWOOD PETALS

DESIGNER: CARMEN JORISSEN

YARN

A - Brown (Copenhagen 066)

B - Navy Blue (Philadelphia 007)

NEEDLES

US size 2.5 (3mm) needles, or as needed to achieve gauge (tension)

GAUGE (TENSION)

31 sts x 30 rows = 4 x 4in (10 x 10cm) square

FINISHED SIZE

5¾ x 5¾in (14.5 x 14.5cm)

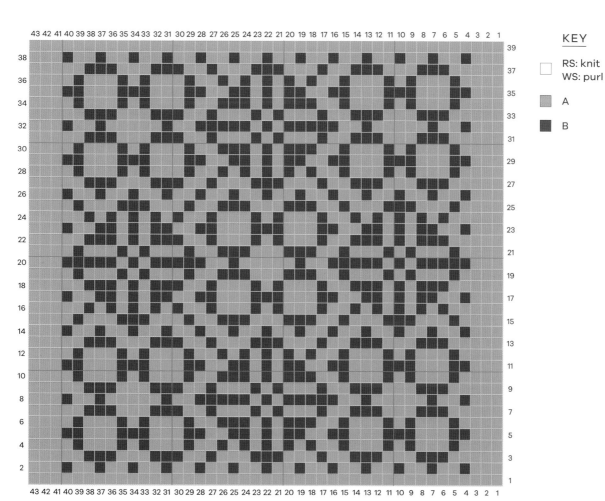

KEY

☐ RS: knit
WS: purl

▨ A

▩ B

NOTES

This tile is worked in stockinette (stocking) stitch following the colourwork chart. The colour not in use should be stranded loosely across the back of the colour being used (see Techniques: Stranded Colourwork).

To make your colourwork look neat, wrap yarn B at the start of every row, preferably on the second stitch, as follows:

On RS rows, insert RH needle into next stitch (to be worked in yarn A), lay yarn B horizontally from right to left over RH needle, knit the stitch using yarn A. Yarn B is now wrapped. Make sure yarn B is not being pulled through the stitch.

On WS rows, insert RH needle into next stitch (to be worked in yarn A), hold yarn B up so that it lays vertically across RH needle, purl the stitch using yarn A.

PATTERN

Using yarn A, cast on 43 sts.

Set-Up Row (WS): Using yarn A, purl to end.

Join in yarn B.

Work Rows 1 to 39 of chart.

Cut yarn B.

Next Row (WS): Using yarn A, purl to end.

Bind (cast) off all sts using yarn A.

Weave in ends and block to finished size.

KITE FLYING

DESIGNER: ANNI HOWARD

YARN

A - Cream (Lyon 078)

B - Orange (Quebec 077)

NEEDLES

US size 3 (3.25mm) needles, or as needed to achieve gauge (tension)

GAUGE (TENSION)

34 sts x 64 rows = 4 x 4in (10 x 10cm) square

FINISHED SIZE

6 x 6in (15 x 15cm)

NOTES

Work this tile using mosaic knitting (see Techniques: Mosaic Knitting). Each chart row represents one RS row and one WS row. Knit stitches that are the colour of the first stitch of the row, and slip the other colour.

PATTERN

Using yarn A, cast on 52 sts.

Work from chart as follows:

Row 1 (RS): Using yarn A, knit to end.

Row 1 (WS): Using yarn A, knit to end.

Row 2 (RS): Using yarn B, [k1, slip 1 purlwise] 14 times, k24.

Row 2 (WS): Using yarn B, k24, [move yarn to front, slip 1 purlwise, move yarn to back, k1] 14 times.

Continue working from chart until Row 48 WS has been completed.

Bind (cast) off all sts knitwise using yarn B.

Weave in ends and block to finished size.

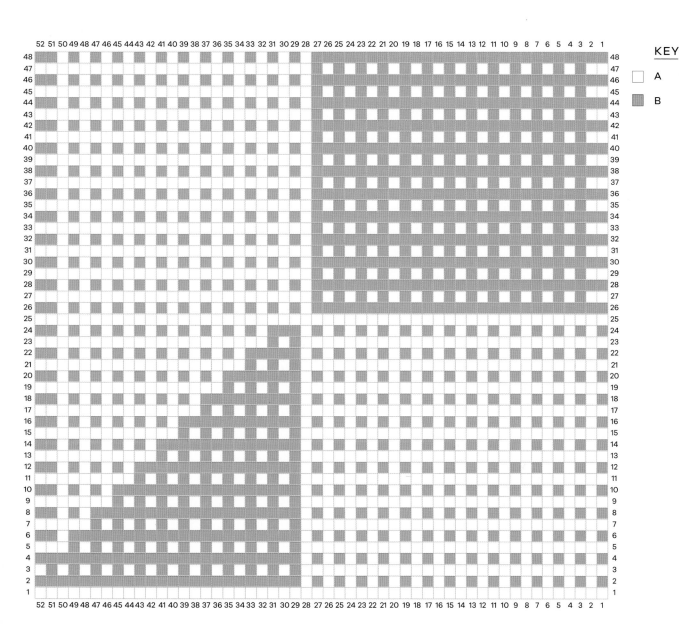

KEY

☐ A

▨ B

TRIANA

DESIGNER: KARIE WESTERMANN

YARN

A - Teal Green (Pasay 022)

B - Light Grey (Cota 024)

C - Medium Blue (Lahore 014)

D - Dark Blue (Boston 011)

NEEDLES

US size 2 (2.75mm) DPNs, or as needed to achieve gauge (tension)

ACCESSORIES

4 stitch markers, including one distinct for BOR

GAUGE (TENSION)

24 sts x 42 rounds = 4 x 4in (10 x 10cm) square

FINISHED SIZE

7 x 7in (18 x 18cm)

NOTES

This tile is worked in the round from the centre to the outer edge.

When working the chart, the colour not in use should be stranded loosely across the back of the colour being used (see Techniques: Stranded Colourwork).

PATTERN

Using yarn A and leaving a long tail, cast on 8 sts. Join to work in the round, being careful not to twist the sts. Mark the beginning of the round. 8 sts

Knit 1 round.

Round 1: [K1, m1L] eight times. 16 sts

Round 2: [K4, place marker] four times, with final marker for BOR.

Round 3: [K1, m1L, k3, m1L] four times. 24 sts

Round 4: Knit.

Round 5: [K1, m1L, k5, m1L] four times. 32 sts

Round 6: Knit.

Round 7: [K1, m1L, k7, m1L] four times. 40 sts

Round 8: Knit.

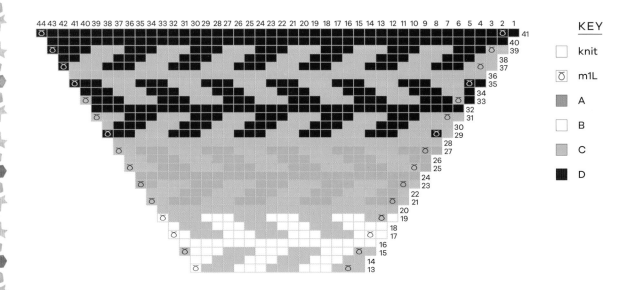

KEY

☐ knit

⟳ m1L

▨ A

☐ B

▨ C

■ D

Round 9: [K1, m1L, k9, m1L] four times. 48 sts

Round 10: Knit.

Round 11: [K1, m1L, k11, m1L] four times. 56 sts

Round 12: Knit.

Join in yarn B.

Repeating chart four times in each round, work Rows 13 to 41 of chart, increasing before and after markers on rounds as indicated. 176 sts

Cut all yarns except yarn D.

Bind (cast) off as follows: K2, *slip 2 sts back to LH needle, k2tog tbl, k1; rep from * to last 2 sts, k2tog tbl.

Fasten off, pulling yarn through last st.

Use the cast-on yarn tail to close the hole at the centre if needed. Weave in ends and block to finished size.

CABLE HEART

· ·

DESIGNER: LYNNE ROWE

YARN

Teal (Suwon 018)

NEEDLES

US size 2.5 (3mm) needles, or as needed to achieve gauge (tension)

ACCESSORIES

Cable needle

GAUGE (TENSION)

30 sts x 43 rows = 4 x 4in (10 x 10cm) square

FINISHED SIZE

6 x 6in (15 x 15cm)

NOTES

The motif is formed by cable stitches (see Special Abbreviations) on a reverse stockinette (stocking) stitch background inside a stockinette (stocking) stitch border.

SPECIAL ABBREVIATIONS

2/2 RC: 2 over 2 right cross – slip 2 sts to cable needle, hold at back of work, k2 from LH needle, k2 from cable needle

2/2 LC: 2 over 2 left cross – slip 2 sts to cable needle, hold at front of work, k2 from LH needle, k2 from cable needle

2/1 RPC: 2 over 1 right cross with purl – slip 1 st to cable needle, hold at back of work, k2 from LH needle, p1 from cable needle

2/1 LPC: 2 over 1 left cross with purl – slip 2 sts to cable needle, hold at front of work, p1 from LH needle, k2 from cable needle

2/2 LPC: 2 over 2 left cross with purl – slip 2 sts to cable needle, hold at front of work, p2 from LH needle, k2 from cable needle

2/2 RPC: 2 over 2 right cross with purl – slip 2 sts to cable needle, hold at back of work, k2 from LH needle, p2 from cable needle

SNOWY MOUNTAIN

DESIGNER: ANNI HOWARD

YARN

A - Cream (Lyon 078)

B - Blue (Lahore 014)

NEEDLES

US size 3 (3.25mm) needles, or as needed to achieve gauge (tension)

GAUGE (TENSION)

34 sts x 64 rows = 4 x 4in (10 x 10cm) square

FINISHED SIZE

6 x 6in (15 x 15cm)

NOTES

Work this tile using mosaic knitting (see Techniques: Mosaic Knitting). Each chart row represents one RS row and one WS row. Knit stitches that are the colour of the first stitch of the row, and slip the other colour.

PATTERN

Cast on 44 sts.

Row 1 (RS): K7, p13, k4, p13, k7.

Row 2: P7, k13, p4, k13, p7.

Row 3: K7, p13, 2/2 RC, p13, k7.

Row 4: Rep Row 2.

Rows 5 to 20: Rep Rows 1 to 4 four times.

Row 21: K7, p12, 2/1 RPC, 2/1 LPC, p12, k7.

Row 22: P7, k12, p2, k2, p2, k12, p7.

Row 23: K7, p11, 2/1 RPC, p2, 2/1 LPC, p11, k7.

Row 24: P7, k11, p2, k4, p2, k11, p7.

Row 25: K7, p10, 2/1 RPC, p4, 2/1 LPC, p10, k7.

Row 26: P7, k10, p2, k6, p2, k10, p7.

Row 27: K7, p9, 2/1 RPC, p6, 2/1 LPC, p9, k7.

Row 28: P7, k9, p2, k8, p2, k9, p7.

Row 29: K7, p8, 2/1 RPC, p8, 2/1 LPC, p8, k7.

Row 30: P7, k8, p2, k10, p2, k8, p7.

Row 31: K7, p7, 2/1 RPC, p10, 2/1 LPC, p7, p7.

Row 32: P7, k7, p2, k12, p2, k7, p7.

Row 33: K7, p6, 2/1 RPC, p12, 2/1 LPC, p6, k7.

Row 34: P7, k6, p2, k14, p2, k6, p7.

Row 35: K7, p5, 2/1 RPC, p14, 2/1 LPC, p5, k7.

Row 36: P7, k5, [p2, k4] three times, p2, k5, p7.

Row 37: K7, p5, k2, p4, 2/2 LPC, 2/2 RPC, p4, k2, p5, k7.

Row 38: P7, k5, p2, k6, p4, k6, p2, k5, p7.

Row 39: K7, p5, k2, p6, k4, p6, k2, p5, k7.

Row 40: Rep Row 38.

Row 41: K7, p5, [2/1 LPC, p4, 2/1 RPC] twice, p5, k7.

Row 42: P7, k6, p2, k4, p6, k4, p2, k6, p7.

Row 43: K7, p6, 2/2 LPC, 2/2 RC, k2, 2/2 LC, 2/2 RPC, p6, k7.

Row 44: P7, k8, p4, k1, p4, k1, p4, k8, p7.

Row 45: K7, p8, 2/2 RPC, p1, 2/2 RC, p1, 2/2 LPC, p8. k7.

Row 46: Rep Row 2.

Rows 47 to 62: Rep Rows 1 to 4 four times.

Rows 63 and 64: Rep Rows 1 and 2.

Bind (cast) off all sts.

Weave in ends and block to finished size.

PATTERN

Using yarn A, cast on 51 sts.

Work from chart as follows:

Row 1 (RS): Using yarn A, knit to end.

Row 1 (WS): Using yarn A, knit to end.

Row 2 (RS): Using yarn B, k2, *slip 1 purlwise, k1; rep from * to last st, k1.

Row 2 (WS): Using yarn B, k2, *move yarn to front, slip 1 purlwise, move yarn to back, k1; rep from * to last st, k1.

Continue working from chart until Row 48 WS has been completed.

Bind (cast) off all sts knitwise using yarn B.

Weave in ends and block to finished size.

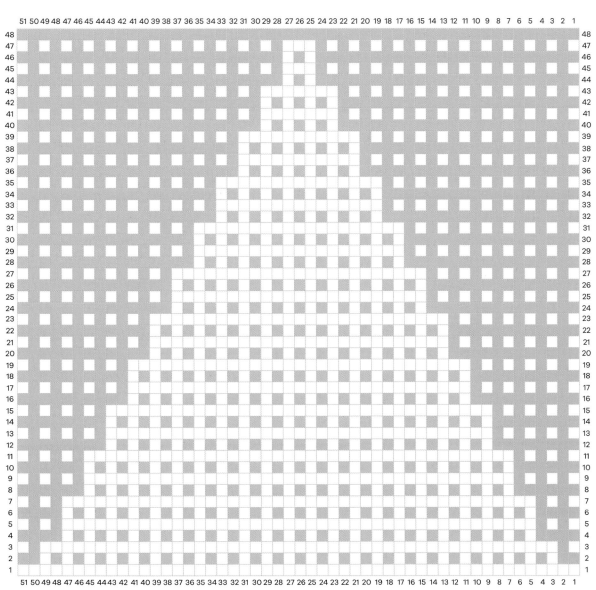

KEY

☐ A

▨ B

AEGEAN SUMMER

DESIGNER: SUZY RAI

YARN

A - Yellow (Atlanta 033)

B - Light Grey (Cota 024)

C - Blue (Lahore 014)

D - Black (Miami 069)

NEEDLES

US size 2.5 (3mm) needles, or as
needed to achieve gauge (tension)

GAUGE (TENSION)

30 sts x 40 rows = 4 x 4in (10 x 10cm)
square

FINISHED SIZE

5½ x 5½in (14 x 14cm)

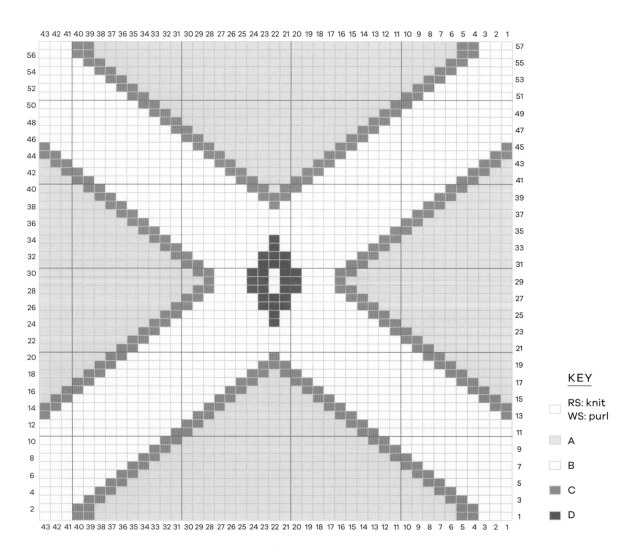

KEY

RS: knit
WS: purl

A

B

C

D

NOTES

The chart is worked in stockinette (stocking) stitch throughout. Use a separate small ball of yarn for each colour section and twist the yarns to avoid a hole (see Techniques: Intarsia).

PATTERN

Using yarn B, cast on 43 sts.

Join in other colours as needed.

Work Rows 1 to 57 of chart.

Bind (cast) off all sts using yarn B.

Weave in ends and block to finished size.

VENATION

DESIGNER: ANNIKEN ALLIS

YARN
Pink (Marrakech 051)

NEEDLES
US size 4 (3.5mm) needles, or as needed to achieve gauge (tension)

GAUGE (TENSION)
22 sts x 30.5 rows = 4 x 4in (10 x 10cm) square

FINISHED SIZE
5½ x 5in (14 x 12.5cm)

NOTES

This tile is worked with a garter stitch border.

Rows 1 to 8 are also shown in the chart.

PATTERN

Cast on 31 sts.

Work 3 rows of garter stitch.

Row 1 (RS): K1, *k4, k2tog, [k1, yo] twice, k1, ssk, k3; rep from * to last 2 sts, k2.

Rows 2, 4 and 6 (WS): K2, purl to last 2 sts, k2.

Row 3: K1, *k3, k2tog, k1, yo, k3, yo, k1, ssk, k2; rep from * to last 2 sts, k2.

Row 5: K1, *k2, k2tog, k1, yo, k5, yo, k1, ssk, k1; rep from * to last 2 sts, k2.

Row 7: K1, *k1, k2tog, k1, yo, k7, yo, k1, ssk; rep from * to last 2 sts, k2.

Row 8 (WS): Rep Row 2.

Rep Rows 1 to 8 three more times.

Work 3 rows of garter stitch.

Bind (cast) off all sts knitwise.

Weave in ends and block to finished size.

PULSAR

DESIGNER: ARELLA SEATON

YARN

A - Dark Blue (Bucharest 001)

B - Yellow (Brasov 038)

NEEDLES

US size 2.5 (3mm) needles, or as needed to achieve gauge (tension)

GAUGE (TENSION)

31 sts x 60 rows = 4 x 4in (10 x 10cm) square

FINISHED SIZE

6 x 6in (15 x 15cm)

NOTES

Work this tile using mosaic knitting (see Techniques: Mosaic Knitting). Each chart row represents one RS row and one WS row. Knit stitches that are the colour of the first stitch of the row, and slip the other colour.

KEY

☐	RS: knit WS: purl
Ⓞ	yo
╲	ssk
╱	k2tog
☐	repeat

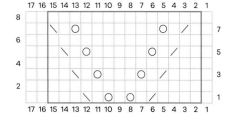

PATTERN

Using yarn A, cast on 47 sts.

Work from chart as follows:

Row 1 (RS): Using yarn A, knit to end.

Row 1 (WS): Using yarn A, knit to end.

Row 2 (RS): Using yarn B, k1, *slip 1 purlwise, k1; rep from * to end.

Row 2 (WS): Using yarn B, k1, *move yarn to front, slip 1 purlwise, move yarn to back, k1; rep from * to end.

Continue working from chart until Row 45 WS has been completed.

Bind (cast) off all sts knitwise using yarn A.

Weave in ends and block to finished size.

KEY

■ A

□ B

AUTUMN COLOUR

DESIGNER: HELEN BIRCH

YARN

A - Beige (Buenos Aires 067)

B - Bright Orange (Tripoli 074)

C - Dark Orange (Liverpool 065)

D - Red (Naples 043)

NEEDLES

US size 2.5 (3mm) needles, or as needed to achieve gauge (tension)

GAUGE (TENSION)

32 sts x 60 rows = 4 x 4in (10 x 10cm) square

FINISHED SIZE

6 x 6in (15 x 15cm)

NOTES

Slip all stitches purlwise with the yarn held at the wrong side of the work (slipping with yarn in back on RS rows and with yarn in front on WS rows).

PATTERN

Using yarn B, cast on 47 sts.

Knit 2 rows.

Join in yarn A.

Row 1 (RS): Using yarn A, k1, *slip 1, k1; rep from * to end.

Row 2: Using yarn A, p1, *slip 1, p1; rep from * to end.

Row 3: Using yarn B, slip 1, *k1, slip 1; rep from * to end.

Row 4: Using yarn B, slip 1, *p1, slip 1; rep from * to end.

Rows 5 to 16: Rep Rows 1 to 4 three times.

Cut yarn B and join in yarn C as needed.

Row 17: Using yarn A, k1, *slip 1, k1; rep from * to end.

Row 18: Using yarn A, p1, *slip 1, p1; rep from * to end.

Row 19: Using yarn C, slip 1, *k1, slip 1; rep from * to end.

Row 20: Using yarn C, slip 1, *p1, slip 1; rep from * to end.

Rows 21 to 32: Rep Rows 17 to 20 three times.

Cut yarn C and join in yarn D as needed.

Row 33: Using yarn A, k1, *slip 1, k1; rep from * to end.

Row 34: Using yarn A, p1, *slip 1, p1; rep from * to end.

Row 35: Using yarn D, slip 1, *k1, slip 1; rep from * to end.

Row 36: Using yarn D, slip 1, *p1, slip 1; rep from * to end.

Rows 37 to 48: Rep Rows 33 to 36 three times.

Cut yarn D and join in yarn C as needed.

Rows 49 to 64: Rep Rows 17 to 20 four times.

Cut yarn C and join in yarn B as needed.

Rows 65 to 80: Rep Rows 1 to 4 four times.

Cut yarn A and continue with yarn B only.

Knit 3 rows.

Bind (cast) off all sts knitwise.

SIDE BORDERS (BOTH ALIKE)

With RS facing, and yarn B, starting at one corner pick up and knit 42 sts along row ends to next corner.

Knit 2 rows.

Bind (cast) off knitwise.

FINISHING

Weave in ends and block to finished size.

RUBIES

DESIGNER: ANNAPLEXIS

YARN

A - Red (Naples 043)

B - Yellow (Dhaka 040)

NEEDLES

US size 1.5 (2.5mm) needles, or as
needed to achieve gauge (tension)

GAUGE (TENSION)

29 sts x 45 rows = 4 x 4in (10 x 10cm)
square

FINISHED SIZE

6¼ x 5½in (16 x 14cm)

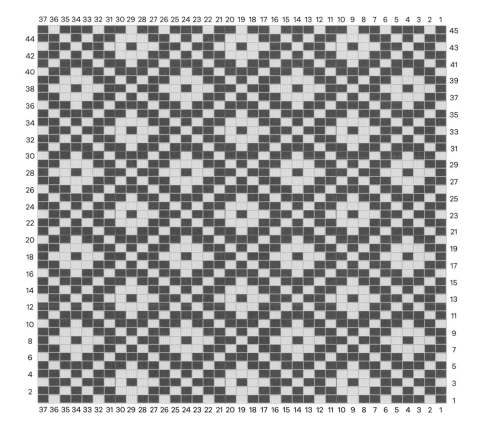

KEY

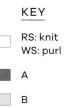

☐ RS: knit
WS: purl

■ A

☐ B

NOTES

This tile is knitted with a garter stitch border. The chart is worked in stockinette (stocking) stitch.

When working with two colours at once, the colours not in use should be stranded loosely across the back of the colour being used (see Techniques: Stranded Colourwork).

Slip the first stitch of each row purlwise.

PATTERN

Using yarn A, cast on 45 sts.

Next Row: Slip 1, knit to end.

Rep this row four more times.

Join in yarn B and work as follows:

Row 1 (RS): Slip 1, k3 using yarn A, knit Row 1 of chart, k4 using yarn A.

Row 2: Slip 1, k3 using yarn A, purl Row 2 of chart, k4 using yarn A.

Keeping first 4 sts and last 4 sts in garter stitch as set using yarn A throughout, continue until chart is complete.

Cut yarn B and continue with yarn A only.

Next Row: Using yarn A, slip 1, knit to end.

Rep this row five more times.

Bind (cast) off all sts.

Weave in ends and block to finished size.

TILTED

DESIGNER: ANNI HOWARD

YARN

A - Orange (Quebec 077)

B - Blue (Lahore 014)

C - Cream (Lyon 078)

NEEDLES

US size 3 (3.25mm) needles, or as needed to achieve gauge (tension)

GAUGE (TENSION)

34 sts x 64 rows = 4 x 4in (10 x 10cm) square

FINISHED SIZE

6 x 6in (15 x 15cm)

NOTES

Work this tile using mosaic knitting (see Techniques: Mosaic Knitting). Each chart row represents one RS row and one WS row. Knit stitches that are the colour of the first stitch of the row, and slip the other colour.

Starting from Row 5, also use intarsia (see Techniques: Intarsia), with each block of colour knit from a separate ball or bobbin of yarn. Twist the working yarns at the colour changes of yarn A and yarn C to avoid holes. You can work from one ball of yarn B as this is used across the entire row each time.

PATTERN

Using yarn A, cast on 51 sts.

Work from chart as follows:

Row 1 (RS): Using yarn A, knit to end.

Row 1 (WS): Using yarn A, knit to end.

Row 2 (RS): Using yarn B, k1, *slip 1 purlwise, k1; rep from * to end.

Row 2 (WS): Using yarn B, k1, *move yarn to front, slip 1 purlwise, move yarn to back, k1; rep from * to end.

Continue working from chart until Row 49 WS has been completed, joining yarn C and a separate ball of yarn A in Row 5 and cutting yarn C after Row 45.

Bind (cast) off all sts knitwise using yarn A.

Weave in ends and block to finished size.

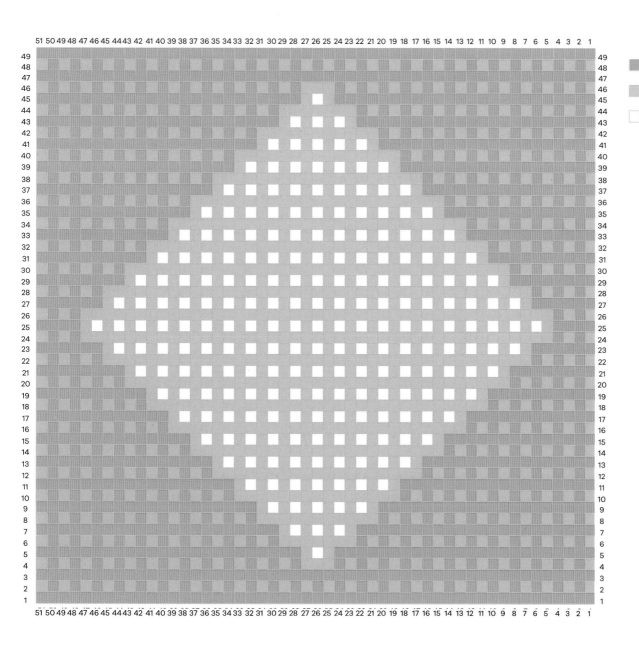

KEY

A

B

C

HOURGLASS

DESIGNER: JACQUI GOULBOURN

YARN

Pink (Montreal 059)

NEEDLES

US size 2 (2.75mm) needles, or as needed to achieve gauge (tension)

GAUGE (TENSION)

30 sts x 40 rows = 4 x 4in (10 x 10cm) square

FINISHED SIZE

6 x 6in (15 x 15cm)

NOTES

The eyelet stitch is worked over 3 stitches as follows: Pass the third st on LH needle over the first two sts and off the needle, then work k1 tbl, yo, k1 tbl.

Row 32 is the centre point of the pattern. Once you have completed Row 32, work from Row 31 to Row 1 in reverse order. All rows are also shown in the chart.

PATTERN

Cast on 47 sts.

Row 1 (RS): Knit.

Row 2: P1, k45, p1.

Row 3: K1, p1, k43, p1, k1.

Row 4: P1, k1, p1, k41, p1, k1, p1.

Row 5: [K1, p1] twice, k1, [p1, k1 tbl] 18 times, [p1, k1] three times.

Row 6: [P1, k1] twice, p1, [k1, p1 tbl] 18 times, [k1, p1] three times.

Row 7: [K1, p1] twice, k2, [eyelet, p1] eight times, eyelet, k2, [p1, k1] twice.

Row 8: [P1, k1] twice, p3, [k1, p1 tbl] 16 times, k1, p3, [k1, p1] twice.

Row 9: [K1, p1] twice, k3, [p1, k1 tbl] 16 times, p1, k3, [p1, k1] twice.

Row 10: [P1, k1] twice, p3, [k1, p1 tbl] 16 times, k1, p3, [k1, p1] twice.

Row 11: [K1, p1] twice, k4, [eyelet, p1] seven times, eyelet, k4, [p1, k1] twice.

Row 12: [P1, k1] twice, p5, [k1, p1 tbl] 14 times, k1, p5, [k1, p1] twice.

Row 13: [K1, p1] twice, k5, [p1, k1 tbl] 14 times, p1, k5, [p1, k1] twice.

Row 14: [P1, k1] twice, p5, [k1, p1 tbl] 14 times, k1, p5, [k1, p1] twice.

Row 15: [K1, p1] twice, k6, [eyelet, p1] six times, eyelet, k6, [p1, k1] twice.

Row 16: [P1, k1] twice, p7, [k1, p1 tbl] 12 times, k1, p7, [k1, p1] twice.

Row 17: [K1, p1] twice, k7, [p1, k1 tbl] 12 times, p1, k7, [p1, k1] twice.

Row 18: [P1, k1] twice, p7, [k1, p1 tbl] 12 times, k1, p7, [k1, p1] twice.

Row 19: [K1, p1] twice, k8, [eyelet, p1] five times, eyelet, k8, [p1, k1] twice.

Row 20: [P1, k1] twice, p9, [k1, p1 tbl] ten times, k1, p9, [k1, p1] twice.

Row 21: [K1, p1] twice, k9, [p1, k1 tbl] ten times, p1, k9, [p1, k1] twice.

Row 22: [P1, k1] twice, p9, [k1, p1 tbl] ten times, k1, p9, [k1, p1] twice.

Row 23: [K1, p1] twice, k10, [eyelet, p1] four times, eyelet, k10, [p1, k1] twice.

Row 24: [P1, k1] twice, p11, [k1, p1 tbl] eight times, k1, p11, [k1, p1] twice.

Row 25: [K1, p1] twice, k11, [p1, k1 tbl] eight times, p1, k11, [p1, k1] twice.

Row 26: [P1, k1] twice, p11, [k1, p1 tbl] eight times, k1, p11, [k1, p1] twice.

Row 27: [K1, p1] twice, k12, [eyelet, p1] three times, eyelet, k12, [p1, k1] twice.

Row 28: [P1, k1] twice, p13, [k1, p1 tbl] six times, k1, p13, [k1, p1] twice.

Row 29: [K1, p1] twice, k13, [p1, k1 tbl] six times, p1, k13, [p1, k1] twice.

Row 30: [P1, k1] twice, p13, [k1, p1 tbl] six times, k1, p13, [k1, p1] twice.

Row 31: [K1, p1] twice, k14, [eyelet, p1] twice, eyelet, k14, [p1, k1] twice.

Row 32: [P1, k1] twice, p14, [p1 tbl, k1] five times, p1 tbl, p14, [k1, p1] twice.

Rows 33 to 63: Rep Rows 31 through Row 1 in reverse order (e.g. rep Row 31, then Row 30, then Row 29, and so forth until you end with Row 1).

Bind (cast) off all sts knitwise.

Weave in ends and block to finished size.

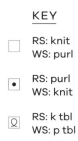

KEY

☐	RS: knit WS: purl
•	RS: purl WS: knit
Ⓠ	RS: k tbl WS: p tbl
Ⓠ ○ Ⓠ	eyelet

PORTHOLE

DESIGNER: ANNI HOWARD

YARN

A - Cream (Lyon 078)

B - Orange (Quebec 077)

NEEDLES

US size 3 (3.25mm) needles, or as
needed to achieve gauge (tension)

GAUGE (TENSION)

34 sts x 64 rows = 4 x 4in (10 x 10cm)
square

FINISHED SIZE

6 x 6in (15 x 15cm)

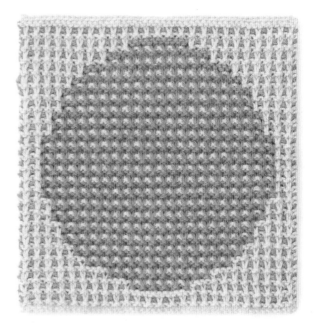

KEY

☐ A

▨ B

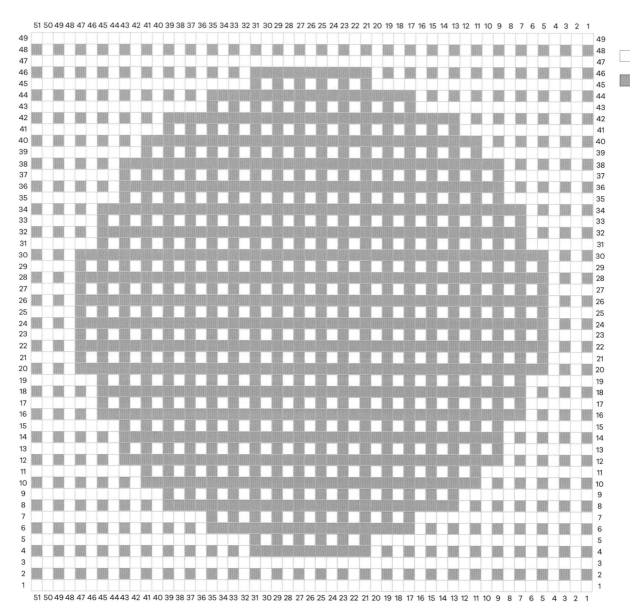

NOTES

Work this tile using mosaic knitting (see Techniques: Mosaic Knitting). Each chart row represents one RS row and one WS row. Knit stitches that are the colour of the first stitch of the row, and slip the other colour.

PATTERN

Using yarn A, cast on 51 sts.

Work from chart as follows:

Row 1 (RS): Using yarn A, knit to end.

Row 1 (WS): Using yarn A, knit to end.

Row 2 (RS): Using yarn B, k1, *slip 1 purlwise, k1; rep from * to end.

Row 2 (WS): Using yarn B, k1, *move yarn to front, slip 1 purlwise, move yarn to back, k1; rep from * to end.

Continue working from chart until Row 49 WS has been completed.

Bind (cast) off all sts knitwise using yarn A.

Weave in ends and block to finished size.

AWASH

DESIGNER: ANNA NIKIPIROWICZ

YARN

A - Grey (Izmir 073)

B - Green (Canberra 031)

C - Blue (Lahore 014)

D - Pink (Montreal 059)

NEEDLES

US size 4 (3.5mm) needles, or as needed to achieve gauge (tension)

GAUGE (TENSION)

25 sts x 48 rows = 4 x 4in (10 x 10cm) square

FINISHED SIZE

Point to point: 6¼ x 6¼in (16 x 16cm)

NOTES

This tile is worked from one corner to the other with increases to the centre point, then decreases to shape the second half. The pattern is formed from the stripes of colour and a textured pattern with garter stitch edging worked as you go. Slip stitches purlwise with yarn held at back of work.

PATTERN

Using yarn A, cast on 3 sts.

INCREASE SECTION

Rows 1 and 2: Knit.

Row 3 (RS): k1, [kfb] twice. 5 sts

Row 4: Knit.

Row 5: K1, m1L, knit to last st, m1L, k1. 7 sts

Row 6: K2, p3, p2.

Change to yarn B.

Row 7 (RS): K1, m1L, [k1, slip 1] twice, k1, m1L, k1. 2 sts increased

Row 8: K3, [slip 1, k1] twice, k2.

Row 9: K1, m1L, knit to last st, m1L, k1. 2 sts increased

Row 10: K2, purl to last 2 sts, k2.

Change to yarn A.

Row 11 (RS): K1, m1L, *k1, slip 1; rep from * to last 2 sts, k1, m1L, k1. 2 sts increased

Row 12: K3, *slip 1, k1; rep from * to last 2 sts, k2.

Row 13: K1, m1L, knit to last st, m1L, k1. 2 sts increased

Row 14: K2, purl to last 2 sts, k2.

Change to yarn B.

Rows 15 to 18: Rep Rows 11 to 14. 4 sts increased

Rows 19 to 44: Rep Rows 11 to 18 twice more, changing colours as before. 35 sts

Rows 45 to 60: Rep Rows 11 to 18 twice more, changing to yarn C instead of yarn B. 51 sts

Rows 61 to 64: Using yarn A, rep Rows 11 to 14. 55 sts

DECREASE SECTION

Change to yarn C.

Row 65 (RS): K1, k2tog, k1, *slip 1, k1; rep from * to last 3 sts, k2tog, k1. 2 sts decreased

Row 66: K3, *slip 1, k1; rep from * to last 2 sts, k2.

Row 67: K1, k2tog, knit to last 3 sts, k2tog, k1. 2 sts decreased

Row 68: K2, purl to last 2 sts, k2.

Change to yarn A.

Rows 69 to 72: Rep Rows 65 to 68. 4 sts decreased

Rows 73 to 80: Rep Rows 65 to 72, changing colours as before. 39 sts

Rows 81 to 112: Rep Rows 65 to 72 four times, changing to yarn D instead of C. 7 sts

Change to yarn A.

Row 113 (RS): K1, [k2tog, k1] twice. 5 sts

Row 114: Knit.

Row 115: K1, k2tog, k2. 4 sts

Row 116: Knit.

Bind (cast) off all sts.

Weave in ends and block to finished size.

DELFT SWALLOWS

DESIGNER: LILY LANGMAN

YARN

A - Cream (Lyon 078)

B - Blue (Washington 013)

NEEDLES

US size 1.5 (2.5mm) needles, or as needed to achieve gauge (tension)

GAUGE (TENSION)

29 sts x 45 rows = 4 x 4in (10 x 10cm) square

FINISHED SIZE

6¾ x 6in (17 x 15cm)

NOTES

This tile is knitted with a border of garter stitch on the top and bottom edges and 3 garter stitches on each side. The chart is worked in stockinette (stocking) stitch.

When working with two or three colours at once, the colours not in use should be stranded loosely across the back of the colour being used (see Techniques: Stranded Colourwork).

When stranding the yarn becomes difficult, use a separate ball of yarn for each colour and twist the yarn about to be used around the colour just used to link yarns together on WS to avoid a hole (see Techniques: Intarsia).

If you prefer to work a smaller tile without the border, cast on 43 sts using yarn A, work the chart, then bind (cast) off using yarn A.

PATTERN

Using yarn A, cast on 49 sts.

Work 4 rows of garter stitch.

Join in yarn B as needed and work as follows:

Row 1 (RS): K3 using yarn A, knit Row 1 of chart, k3 using yarn A.

Row 2: K3 using yarn A, purl Row 2 of chart, k3 using yarn A.

Keeping first 3 sts and last 3 sts in garter stitch using yarn A throughout, continue until chart is complete.

Cut yarn B.

Work 3 rows of garter stitch using yarn A.

Bind (cast) off all sts.

Weave in ends and block to finished size.

KEY

☐ RS: knit
  WS: purl

☐ A

■ B

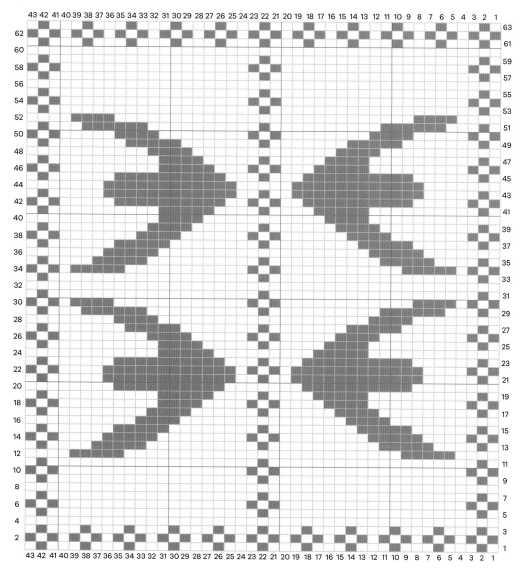

GEOMETRICA

DESIGNER: ANNAPLEXIS

YARN

A - Purple (Santiago 053)

B - Pale Yellow (Delhi 039)

NEEDLES

US size 1.5 (2.5mm) DPNs, or as needed to achieve gauge (tension)

ACCESSORIES

4 stitch markers, including one distinct for BOR

GAUGE (TENSION)

29 sts x 45 rounds = 4 x 4in (10 x 10cm) square

FINISHED SIZE

6¼ x 6¼in (16 x 16cm)

NOTES

This tile is worked in the round from the outer edge to the centre, working from the chart and including a garter stitch border.

When working the chart, the colour not in use should be stranded loosely across the back of the colour being used (see Techniques: Stranded Colourwork).

PATTERN

Using yarn A, cast on 180 sts. Join to work in the round, being careful not to twist the sts.

Round 1: [Work Row 1 of chart, place marker] four times, with final marker for BOR.

Continue working as set, slipping markers and working decreases as shown, and joining in yarn B as needed, until chart is complete. 12 sts

Cut both yarn strands and thread tail of yarn A through remaining sts, pulling tight to close the hole.

Weave in ends and block to finished size.

KEY

☐ knit

• purl

/ k2tog

\ ssk

■ A

☐ B

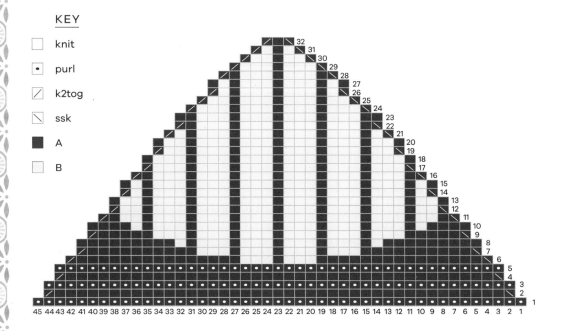

SWIVEL

DESIGNER: ARELLA SEATON

YARN

A - Yellow (Brasov 038)

B - Dark Blue (Bucharest 001)

NEEDLES

US size 2.5 (3mm) needles, or as
needed to achieve gauge (tension)

GAUGE (TENSION)

31 sts x 60 rows = 4 x 4in (10 x 10cm) square

FINISHED SIZE

6¼ x 6¼in (16 x 16cm)

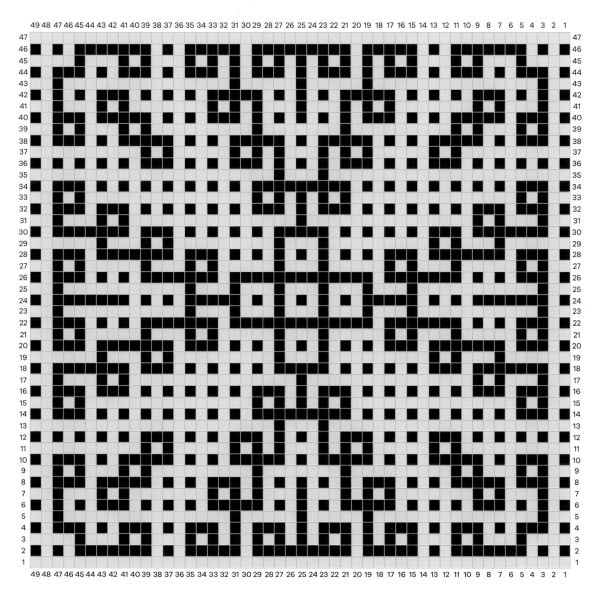

KEY

- ☐ A
- ■ B

NOTES

Work this tile using mosaic knitting (see Techniques: Mosaic Knitting). Each chart row represents one RS row and one WS row. Knit stitches that are the colour of the first stitch of the row, and slip the other colour.

PATTERN

Using yarn A, cast on 49 sts.

Work from chart as follows:

Row 1 (RS): Using yarn A, knit to end.

Row 1 (WS): Using yarn A, knit to end.

Row 2 (RS): Using yarn B, [k1, slip 1 purlwise] twice, k7, slip 1 purlwise, k1, slip 1 purlwise, k5, slip 1 purlwise, k9, slip 1 purlwise, k5, slip 1 purlwise, k1, slip 1 purlwise, k7, [slip 1 purlwise, k1] twice.

Row 2 (WS): Using yarn B, [k1, move yarn to front, slip 1 purlwise, move yarn to back] twice, k7, move yarn to front, slip 1 purlwise, move yarn to back, k1, move yarn to front, slip 1 purlwise, move yarn to back, k5, move yarn to front, slip 1 purlwise, move yarn to back, k9, move yarn to front, slip 1 purlwise, move yarn to back, k5, move yarn to front, slip 1 purlwise, move yarn to back, k1, move yarn to front, slip 1 purlwise, move yarn to back, k7, [move yarn to front, slip 1 purlwise, move yarn to back, k1] twice.

Continue working from chart until Row 47 WS has been completed.

Bind (cast) off all sts knitwise using yarn A.

Weave in ends and block to finished size.

HAPPY GO LUCKY

DESIGNER: LISA MCFETRIDGE

YARN

A - Dark Pink (Montreal 059)

B - Light Pink (Bangalore 052)

NEEDLES

US size 2 (2.75mm) needles, or as needed to achieve gauge (tension)

GAUGE (TENSION)

34 sts x 38 rows = 4 x 4in (10 x 10cm) square

FINISHED SIZE

6 x 6¼in (15 x 16cm)

NOTES

Strand the colour not in use loosely across the back of the colour being used (see Techniques: Stranded Colourwork).

Knit the first and last stitch of every row whether on a RS or WS row, in order to create a tight edge.

PATTERN

Using yarn A, cast on 51 sts in [k1, p1] rib using cable cast on (see Techniques: Cable Cast On).

Join in yarn B as needed.

Work Rows 1 to 61 of chart.

Bind (cast) off all sts firmly in [k1, p1] rib.

Weave in ends and block to finished size.

KEY

☐ RS: knit
   WS: purl

⊡ WS: knit

■ A

▨ B

THE PROJECTS

THROUGH BAG

DESIGNER: JOANNE FOWLER

YARN

Light Grey (Cota 024); 4 balls

NEEDLES

US size 1.5 (2.5mm) DPNs, or as needed
to achieve gauge (tension)

OTHER TOOLS AND MATERIALS

5 stitch markers, including one distinct
for BOR

Snap fastener, optional

Card or plastic for stiffening, optional

Lining fabric, optional

Interfacing for lining fabric, optional

GAUGE (TENSION)

21 sts x 44 rounds = 4 x 4in (10 x 10cm)
square measured over pattern stitch;
28 sts x 44 rows/rounds = 4 x 4in (10
x 10cm) measured over stockinette
(stocking) stitch

FINISHED SIZE

Bag body: 12 x 12in (30 x 30cm)

Strap and gusset width: 2in (5cm)

Strap length: 24in (61cm)

NOTES

*Eight motif style tiles are knitted and
seamed into two 2 x 2 squares to make
the bag front and back. The base, side
gusset and strap piece is knitted flat,
back and forth as a single long thin
strip. This strip is seamed to both front
and back along the base, up one side,
a length left for the strap, down the
third side of the bag and a second layer
along the base. Optional finishes include
a snap fastener closure, stiffening the
base and top edge, and lining.*

PATTERN

BAG FRONT AND BACK

Using the Through tile pattern instructions, make eight squares.

BASE, SIDE GUSSET AND STRAP

Cast on 15 sts.

Row 1 (RS): Knit.

Row 2: Purl.

Continue to work in stockinette (stocking) stitch by repeating Rows 1 and 2 until piece measures 72in (183cm).

Bind (cast) off all sts.

Weave in ends and block to size.

MAKING UP

Note that finished measurements are given for seaming with mattress stitch for a subtle, flat seam (see Techniques: Mattress Stitch). You can use your preferred seaming method, such as whip stitch (see Techniques: Whip Stitch) or a crochet join from the wrong side, though these techniques may result in a slightly smaller bag and longer strap.

Seam four tiles into a square of two tiles by two tiles for the bag front. Repeat to create the bag back.

Overlap the ends of the base, side gusset and strap piece by 12in (30cm), this is the bag base width.

Seam both layers of the doubled section along one side of the bag front piece and the other side of the doubled section to the bag back piece.

Without stretching either piece, continue to seam the long strip along each side of the front and back pieces, securing well at the top edges.

Allow both sides of the handle to roll in using the natural curl of stockinette (stocking) stitch and secure the central bag base by stitching where the piece ends overlap.

OPTIONAL

You could add a snap fastener just inside the top edge of the bag at the centre.

If you prefer a sturdier, less flexible base, place a 12 x 2in (30 x 5cm) strip of card or plastic between the overlapping base two layers and seam the outer opening closed. If you are sure you don't want to stiffen the base, seam the inner opening closed too.

If you prefer the top edges of the bag front and back to be less stretchy, work a back stitch or strip of surface crochet from the wrong side just inside the edge.

If you prefer a lined bag, you can create a lining as follows:

Choose your fabric depending on whether you prefer your bag to retain its stretchiness - a woven fabric will hold the shape while a fabric such as jersey will keep the bag stretchy. Also keep in mind that the wrong side of your fabric will be visible through the eyelets.

Draw two squares of 12 x 12in (30 x 30cm) on the wrong side of your lining fabric and add a ⅝in (1.5cm) seam allowance all round. Draw a strip of 36 x 2in (90 x 5cm) on the wrong side of your lining fabric and add a ⅝in (1.5cm) seam allowance all round.

If you wish, you could add fusible or sew-in interfacing to the strip of fabric.

Cut out all three pieces.

With wrong sides facing, stitch the strip along one long edge to three sides of one square and then along the opposite long edge to three sides of the other square.

Press seams flat so they lie over the strip not the squares, to prevent them being visible through the eyelets. Press the seam allowance on the unseamed edges to the wrong side.

Place the lining in the bag with the wrong side of the fabric facing the knitted piece. Stitch just inside the top edge of the bag, and at a similar level to the strap, taking care not to stretch the knitted piece.

MIX IT CUSHION

DESIGNER: ANNI HOWARD

YARN

A - Orange (Quebec 077); 4 balls

B - Cream (Lyon 078); 1 ball

C - Blue (Lahore 014); 1 ball

NEEDLES

US size 3 (3.25mm) needles, or as needed to achieve mosaic gauge (tension)

US size 6 (4mm) needles, or as needed to achieve garter gauge (tension)

OTHER TOOLS AND MATERIALS

3 buttons, 1¼in (3cm) diameter

Cushion pad, 20 x 20in (51 x 51cm)

GAUGE (TENSION)

34 sts x 64 rows = 4 x 4in (10 x 10cm) square over mosaic patten on US size 3 (3.25mm) needles

24 sts x 45 rows = 4 x 4in (10 x 10cm) square over garter stitch on US size 6 (4mm) needles

FINISHED SIZE

18 x 18in (45 x 45cm)

NOTES

Nine tiles are knitted and seamed into a 3 x 3 square to make the front. The back is worked in garter stitch in two pieces, with buttonholes on upper back.

The cover is designed to have a firm, plump fit; if you prefer a looser cover, you can use a smaller cushion pad.

PATTERN

FRONT

Using the Mix It tile pattern instructions, make nine squares.

Seam tiles together using mattress stitch (see Techniques: Mattress Stitch) using yarn A and following the schematic for placement.

LOWER BACK

Using US size 6 (4mm) needles and yarn A, cast on 108 sts.

Work in garter stitch for 10in (25cm), ending after a RS row.

Bind (cast) off knitwise.

Weave in ends and block to 18 x 10in (45 x 25cm).

UPPER BACK

Using US size 6 (4mm) needles and yarn A, cast on 108 sts.

Work in garter stitch for 8½in (21.5cm), ending after a WS row.

Buttonhole row 1 (RS): K20, [bind (cast) off 2 sts, k31 (including loop on needle after bind-off)] twice, bind (cast) off 2 sts, knit to end.

Buttonhole row 2 (WS): [Knit to gap over bound-off (cast-off) sts, turn, cast on 2 sts using cable method, turn] three times, knit to end.

Continue in garter stitch until work measures 10in (25cm), ending after a RS row.

Bind (cast) off knitwise.

Weave in ends and block to 18 x 10in (45 x 25cm).

MAKING UP

Sew cast-on edge of lower back to bottom edge of front. Sew cast-on edge of upper back to top edge of front.

Overlap back sections so that back measures same as front. Sew on buttons to correspond with buttonholes and fasten. Join lower side seams using mattress stitch. Join upper side seams, making sure to overlap previously sewn lower side seams.

Unfasten buttons and weave in any remaining ends. Insert cushion pad and fasten buttons.

SEVILLA THROW

DESIGNER: ASHLEIGH WEMPE

YARN

A - Medium Orange (Sevilla 076); 10 balls

B - Dark Orange (Mexico City 075);
10 balls

C - Light Grey (Cota 024); 3 balls

D - Dark Blue (Bucharest 001); 2 balls

E - Navy Blue (Philadelphia 007); 2 balls

NEEDLES

US size 8 (5mm) DPNs

US size 7 (4.5mm) DPNs, or as
needed to achieve gauge (tension)

US size 7 (4.5mm) circular needles, 24-
60in (60-150cm) long

ACCESSORIES

4 stitch markers, including one distinct
for BOR

GAUGE (TENSION)

15 sts x 27 rows/rounds = 4 x 4in (10 x
10cm) square using yarn held double on
US size 7 (4.5mm) needles

FINISHED SIZE

54 x 54in (137 x 137cm)

NOTES

*A total of 49 tiles are needed for this
project in seven different patterns/
colours - labelled Tile A through Tile
G. Tiles are joined together as per the
schematic. Then a garter stitch border
is worked around the blanket, one side
at a time.*

PATTERN

TILE A (20 TILES)

Using the Standard tile pattern instructions, make 20 tiles using yarn A and yarn B.

TILE B (10 TILES)

Using the Standard tile pattern instructions, make ten tiles using two strands of yarn B.

TILE C (10 TILES)

Using the Standard tile pattern instructions, make ten tiles using two strands of yarn A.

TILE D (2 TILES)

Using the Romantic Medallion tile pattern instructions, make one tile with two strands of yarn C as MC and one strand each of yarn D and yarn E as CC, then make a second tile with colours reversed, i.e. one strand each of yarn D and yarn E as MC and two strands of yarn C as CC.

TILE E (2 TILES)

Using the Artisan Marvel tile pattern instructions, make one tile with two strands of yarn C as MC and one strand each of yarn D and yarn E as CC, then make a second tile with colours reversed, i.e. one strand each of yarn D and yarn E as MC and two strands of yarn C as CC.

TILE F (2 TILES)

Using the Whimsical Wonder tile pattern instructions, make one tile with two strands of yarn C as MC and one strand each of yarn D and yarn E as CC, then make a second tile with colours reversed, i.e. one strand each of yarn D and yarn E as MC and two strands of yarn C as CC.

TILE G (3 TILES)

Using the Regal Rhythm tile pattern instructions, make one tile with two strands of yarn C as MC and two strands of yarn D as CC, make a second tile with two strands of yarn C as MC and two strands of yarn E as CC, then make a third tile with one strand each of yarn D and yarn E as MC and two strands of yarn C as CC.

MAKING UP

Using whip stitch for a decorative edge (see Techniques: Whip Stitch) between tiles or mattress stitch for an invisible join (see Techniques: Mattress Stitch), seam tiles together with one strand each of yarn A and yarn B held together and following the schematic. Weave in ends.

BORDER

Using one strand each of yarn A and yarn B held together and US size 7 (4.5mm) circular needles, pick up and knit 27 stitches across each tile and 2 to 3 stitches in seam spaces between tiles. Knit 9 rows in garter stitch.

Bind (cast) off all sts.

Work across remaining three sides in same way, picking up and knitting an additional 6 sts along border edges.

FINISHING

Weave in ends and block to finished size.

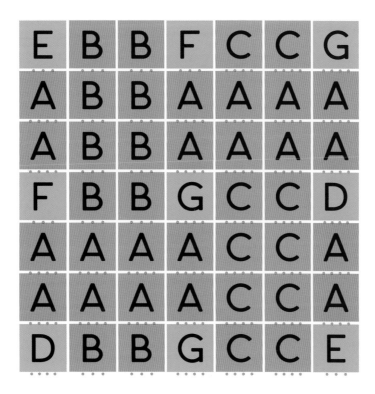

VICTORIAN NEEDLE CASE

DESIGNER: HELEN BIRCH

YARN

A - Cream (Lyon 078)

B - Orange (Tripoli 074)

C - Blue (Boston 011)

D - Red (Naples 043)

NEEDLES

US size 2.5 (3mm) needles, or as needed to achieve gauge (tension)

OTHER TOOLS AND MATERIALS

Felt square, 12 x 12in (30 x 30cm)

Sharp tapestry needle

GAUGE (TENSION)

29 sts x 40 rows = 4 x 4in (10 x 10cm) square

FINISHED SIZE

6½ x 6¾in (16.5 x 17cm)

NOTES

Four tiles are knitted then seamed to create a book shape, with a felt square as the inner 'pages' to hold needles.

The outer spine and case edges are finished with applied i-cord.

Make sure to block tiles before seaming.

PATTERN

INSIDE OF CASE

Using Victorian Diamonds tile pattern instructions, make two tiles.

OUTSIDE OF CASE

Using Victorian Flower tile pattern instructions, make two tiles.

PAGE INSERT - STEP 1

Lay the Victorian Diamonds tiles next to each other with RS facing up as the inside cover of the case. Place the felt square on top and cut to fit inside the tiles.

SPINE SEAM - STEP 2

Fold one half over, sandwiching the layers together.

SPINE SEAM - STEP 3

Sew the spine seam, making sure to secure the felt pages as well as the knitted tiles.

OUTER CASE - STEP 4

Place the Victorian Flower tiles next to each other with WS facing up. Place the inside of the case on top with the Victorian Diamonds tiles opened out and RS down. Tack the knitted pieces together all around the edge.

SPINE I-CORD - STEP 5

With outside of case facing, using yarn C, cast on 5 sts, pick up and knit 1 stitch from spine edge through the outer tiles. Do not turn. 6 sts

Row 1: With RS facing, slip 6 sts onto LH needle. Do not turn.

Row 2: With RS facing, k4, k2tog tbl, pick up and knit next stitch along spine edge. Do not turn.

Repeat Rows 1 to 2, working along spine edge, until you reach end of spine and ending after a Row 1.

Next Row: With RS facing, k4, k2tog tbl, slip 5 sts onto LH needle. Do not turn.

Bind (cast) off.

BORDER I-CORD - STEP 6

With RS facing, using yarn C and starting at spine edge, cast on 5 sts, pick up and knit 1 stitch through outer tiles and spine i-cord. Do not turn. 6 sts

Row 1: With RS facing, slip 6 sts onto LH needle. Do not turn.

Row 2: With RS facing, k4, k2tog tbl, pick up and knit next stitch along edge through both tiles. Do not turn.

Repeat Rows 1 to 2, working along outer edge completely around case and catching the spine i-cord as you pass it, until you reach the starting spine edge again, and ending after a Row 1.

Next Row: With RS facing, k4, k2tog tbl, slip 5 sts onto LH needle. Do not turn.

Bind (cast) off.

FINISHING

Sew cast-on and cast-off ends of border i-cord together.

Weave in ends and block to finished size.

STEP 1 - MAKE PAGE INSERT

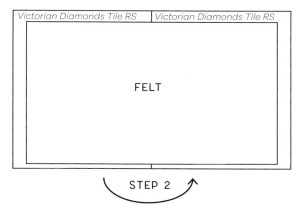

STEP 4 - ADD OUTER CASE

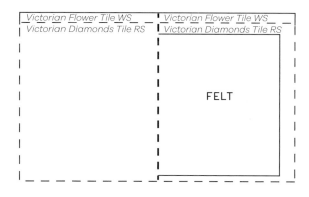

STEP 3 - SEW SPINE SEAM

STEP 5 - SPINE I-CORD

STEP 6 - BORDER I-CORD

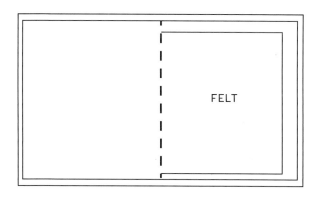

SMOCKED CUSHION

DESIGNER: JACQUI GOULBOURN

YARN

A - Grey (Warsaw 072); 2 balls

B - Pink (Montreal 059); 2 balls

NEEDLES

US size 2 (2.75mm) needles, or as
needed to achieve gauge (tension)

OTHER TOOLS AND MATERIALS

Cable needle

Locking stitch markers

Cushion pad

GAUGE (TENSION)

30 sts x 40 rows = 4 x 4in (10 x 10cm)
square

FINISHED SIZE

15¾ x 15¾in (40 x 40cm)

NOTES

*Eight tiles of each colour are knitted,
then the 16 tiles are seamed into a 4 x 4
checkerboard square. The square is
seamed in such a way that the tiles
show diagonally.*

Make sure to block tiles before seaming.

PATTERN

Using the Smocked tile pattern instructions, make eight squares using yarn A and eight squares using yarn B.

MAKING UP

Lay out the 16 tiles all facing the same way with right sides facing up in a checkerboard square pattern (4 tiles x 4 tiles alternating colours). Before seaming, rotate the tiles of one colour 90 degrees (quarter turn). Every cast-on or bound-off (cast-off) edge will be joined to a side edge of the next tile. Sew the tiles together with whip stitch (see Techniques: Whip Stitch).

When all tiles are joined into a square measuring 24in (60cm), fold the square in half with wrong sides together. Join the short edges on one side together with whip stitch. Repeat for the short edges on the other side.

Rearrange the work to form a square, where the two joined seams now form two halves of a diagonal, and the opening is the perpendicular diagonal.

Insert the cushion pad. You may find it helpful to use locking stitch markers to hold the edges of the opening together as you join together the final seam with whip stitch.

Weave in any remaining ends.

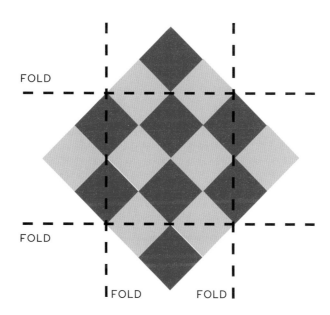

TECHNIQUES

This section includes general techniques used in the tiles and projects in this book. See How to Use This Book for standard abbreviations.

BASIC TECHNIQUES

SLIP KNOT

This knot attaches the yarn to the needle.

Make a loop in the yarn near the end (1). Bring the ball-end of the yarn under the loop and use the tip of the needle to pull it to the front (2). Pull both ends of the yarn to secure the knot around the needle. Do not pull too tightly, leave the slip knot slightly loose (3).

LONG TAIL/CONTINENTAL CAST ON

This method creates an elastic edge.

Measure out about 1in (2.5cm) of yarn for each stitch to be made. Make a slip knot on the left-hand needle at the end of the measured yarn. Wrap the ball-end of the yarn around the index finger and the cut end around the thumb (4). Insert the tip of the right-hand needle up through the loop on the thumb (5). Catch the loop of yarn on the index finger and pull through the loop on the thumb (6). Drop the loop from the thumb and pull tight to form a stitch on the needle (7). Repeat these steps until you have the required number of stitches.

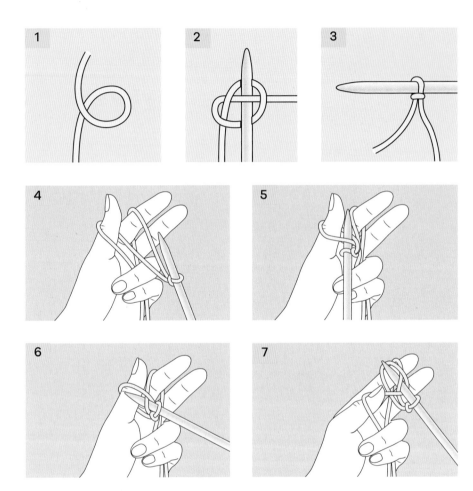

CROCHET PROVISIONAL CAST ON

Using waste yarn and crochet hook, make a few more chains than the total number of stitches required. When selecting waste yarn, look for a piece that is a smooth fibre (such as cotton), and that is slightly thinner than your working yarn.

Then, using the working yarn, pick up and knit stitches in the wrong side of the crochet chain; you will be working into the 'purl bumps' visible on the back of the chain.

When instructed, carefully unpick the waste yarn from the provisional cast-on stitches, placing them onto the needle.

If preferred you can substitute a different provisional cast-on method to end up with the correct number of stitches needed.

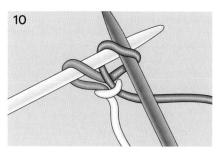

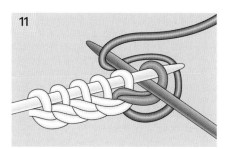

CENTRE-OUT CAST ON

There are several options for centre-out cast-on methods, such as pinhole cast on, disappearing loop cast on, Emily Ocker's cast on or magic ring cast on, some of which require a crochet hook.

The pinhole cast on can be worked with just knitting needles if you want to try a new technique. Make a loop with the working yarn on the top going off to the left. *Put the tip of the needle into the loop from front to back and pull the working yarn through (first stitch), take the needle over the top of the loop and make a yarn over with the working yarn (second stitch); repeat from * to cast on the number of stitches required, then tighten the loop to close the centre hole.

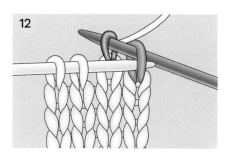

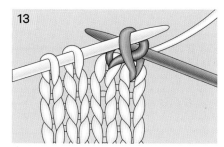

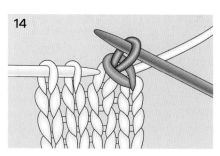

CABLE CAST ON

This method creates a firm edge that is not particularly elastic, suitable for ribbing.

Begin with a slip knot on the needle. Hold the needle with slip knot in your left hand and insert the tip of the needle in your right hand into the slip knot, from front to back.

Take the ball-end of the yarn under the left-hand needle and over the right-hand needle (8). Draw it through the slip knot with the tip of the right-hand needle to make the first stitch (9). Slide the new stitch onto the left-hand needle (10). To make more stitches, slide the right-hand needle between the two stitches on the left-hand needle from front to back, wrap the yarn around the tip of the right-hand needle as before (11). Draw a loop through and place the new stitch on the left-hand needle.

BIND (CAST) OFF

Binding (casting) off can be done knitwise or purlwise, or following a pattern such as in rib.

To bind off knitwise, knit the first stitch, then knit a second stitch. Insert the tip of the left-hand needle into the first stitch (12) and lift it over the second (13) to bind (cast) off the first stitch (14). Knit the next stitch and then lift the previous stitch over it. Repeat until the row is bound (cast) off and there is just one stitch left. Cut the yarn, thread it through the final stitch and tighten.

To bind (cast) off purlwise, work the same way as for knitwise but purl the stitches instead of knitting them.

To bind (cast) off in rib, work the same way as for knitwise but knit all knit stitches and purl all purl stitches.

KNIT STITCH ENGLISH (K)

With the English method the yarn is held in the right hand, at the back of the work, for the knit stitch.

Hold the needle with the stitches in your left hand, with the yarn at the back. Insert the tip of the right-hand needle into the first stitch from front to back and left to right (15). Take the yarn under and around the right-hand needle from left to right (16). Use the tip of the right-hand needle to pull the loop through the stitch on the left-hand needle to form a new stitch on the right-hand needle (17). Slide off the stitch on the left-hand needle (18). Repeat these steps to the end of the row.

KNIT STITCH CONTINENTAL (K)

With the Continental method the yarn is wrapped around the index finger of the left hand, at the back of the work, for the knit stitch.

Insert the tip of the right-hand needle into the first stitch from front to back and left to right (19). Take the yarn over and around the right-hand needle from left to right (20). Use the tip of the right-hand needle to pull the loop through the stitch on the left-hand needle to form a new stitch on the right-hand needle (21). Slide off the stitch on the left-hand needle (22). Repeat these steps to the end of the row.

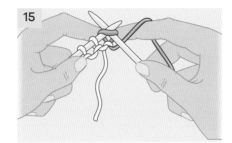

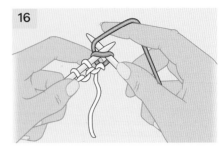

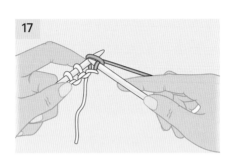

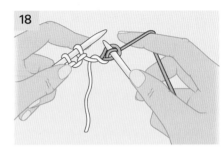

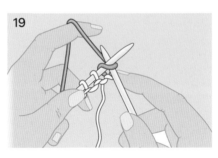

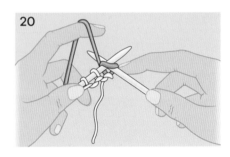

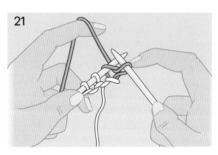

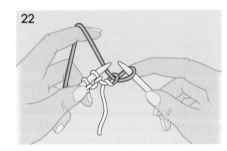

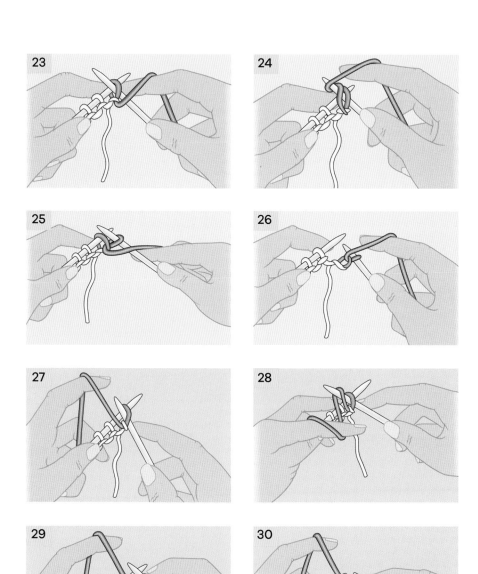

PURL STITCH ENGLISH (P)

With the English method the yarn is held in the right hand, at the front of the work, for the purl stitch.

Hold the needle with the stitches in your left hand, with the yarn at the front. Insert the tip of the right-hand needle into the first stitch from right to left (23). Take the yarn over and around the right-hand needle to form the next stitch (24). Use the tip of the right-hand needle to pull the loop through the stitch on the left-hand needle to form a new stitch on the right-hand needle (25). Slide off the stitch on the left-hand needle (26). Repeat these steps to the end of the row.

PURL STITCH CONTINENTAL (P)

With the Continental method the yarn is wrapped around the index finger of the left hand, at the front of the work, for the purl stitch.

Hold the needle with the stitches in your left hand, with the yarn at the front. Insert the tip of the right-hand needle into the first stitch from right to left (27). Take the yarn over and around the right-hand needle to form the next stitch (28). Use the tip of the right-hand needle to pull the loop through the stitch on the left-hand needle to form a new stitch on the right-hand needle (29). Slide off the stitch on the left-hand needle (30). Repeat these steps to the end of the row.

DECREASING

KNIT TWO STITCHES TOGETHER (K2TOG)

Insert the tip of the right-hand needle into the next two stitches from left to right (1) and knit them as one stitch.

PURL TWO STITCHES TOGETHER (P2TOG)

Insert the tip of the right-hand needle into the next two stitches from right to left (2) and purl them as one stitch.

SLIP ONE, KNIT ONE, PASS SLIPPED STITCH OVER (SKPO)

Slip the first stitch knitwise and knit the second stitch (3). Then pass the slipped stitch over the knitted stitch (4).

SLIP, SLIP, KNIT (SSK)

Slip two stitches knitwise, one at a time (5) onto the right-hand needle. Then knit the two stitches together through the back loops (6).

SLIP ONE, KNIT TWO TOGETHER, PASS SLIPPED STITCH OVER (SK2P)

Slip the first stitch knitwise and then knit the next two stitches together (7). Pass the slipped stitch over the two stitches knitted together (8).

CENTRAL DOUBLE DECREASE (CDD)

Put the tip of the needle into the second and then the first stitch on the left-hand needle knitwise, and slip them together knitwise onto the right-hand needle and then knit the next stitch (9). Pass the slipped stitches over the knit stitch (10).

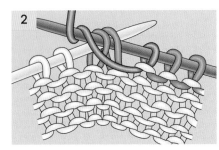

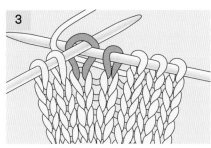
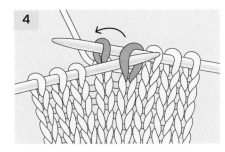

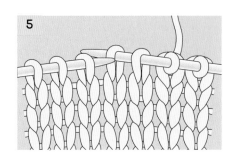
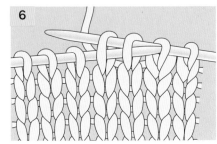

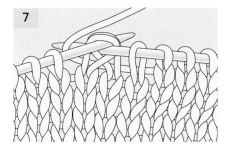
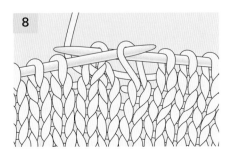

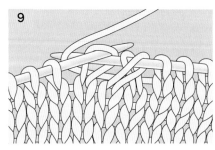
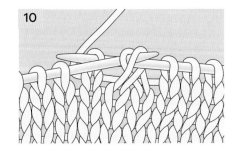

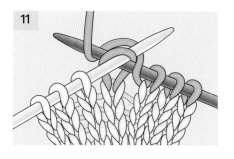

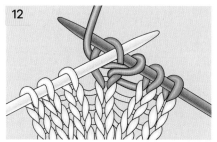

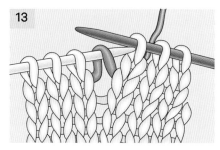

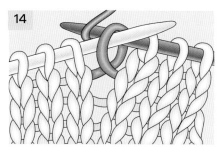

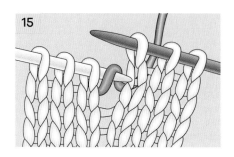

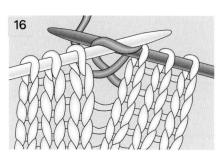

INCREASING

YARN OVER (YO)

Bring the yarn forward and over the needle to the back again (11) and then knit the next stitch.

KNIT FRONT AND BACK (KFB)

Insert the tip of the right-hand needle into the stitch and knit it in the usual way but do not slip it off the needle. Insert the tip of the right-hand needle into the back of the same stitch on the left-hand needle, take the yarn over (12) and knit the stitch again. Now slip the original stitch off the left-hand needle. The increase will show as a bar across the base of the second stitch, so it is easy to count increases.

MAKE ONE LEFT (M1L)

Pick up the bar between two stitches from the front (13), twist it and place on the left-hand needle. Knit into the back loop (14) to increase by one stitch.

MAKE ONE RIGHT (M1R)

Pick up the bar between two stitches from the back (15), twist it and place on the left-hand needle. Knit into the front loop (16) to increase by one stitch.

PICKING UP STITCHES

Insert the right-hand needle into the appropriate space as instructed at the edge of the knitting, from front to back. Loop the yarn around the needle. Pull the yarn through as if to knit and keep the stitch on the right-hand needle. Repeat until the required number of stitches have been picked up.

READING CHARTS

Charts are worked from bottom to top in rows. Each square in a chart represents a stitch or action. The key indicates what each symbol means (what action to take) and, if needed, which yarn to use to perform that action. When working with more than one colour, work the stitch in the yarn colour shown in the chart.

Sections within repeat boxes should be repeated the number of times indicated or to the remaining number of stitches in the row before continuing.

When working back and forth in rows, read RS rows from right to left and read WS rows from left to right. This is indicated by where the row number is located next to the chart – charts worked back and forth in rows have row numbers on both sides of the chart.

When working in the round, read all rows from right to left. Since our tiles worked in the round are also decreasing or increasing, each round may have a different number of stitches than the previous round due to shaping.

When working mosaic, the chart row represents one RS row and one WS row and should be worked with knit and slip stitches as explained in Techniques: Mosaic Knitting. These charts have row numbering on both sides of the chart since you work the RS rows starting from the right and the WS rows starting from the left.

WORKING IN ROWS

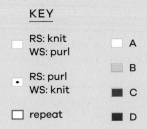

KEY

☐	RS: knit WS: purl	☐	A
⊡	RS: purl WS: knit	▨	B
☐	repeat	■	C
		■	D

WORKING IN THE ROUND

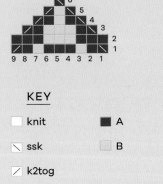

KEY

☐	knit	■	A
◣	ssk	▨	B
◢	k2tog		

WORKING MOSAIC

KEY

☐	A
▨	B
▨	C

COLOURWORK

INTARSIA

Intarsia knitting is used for creating blocks of colour. Use a separate small ball of yarn for each colour. Work along the row until the new colour is needed. Drop the first colour and pick up the second colour underneath the first one, crossing the two yarns over before working the next stitch in the second colour. Crossing the yarns ensures that no holes are created between colours.

MOSAIC KNITTING

Mosaic knitting uses knit and slip sts, working with only one colour in each pair of rows.

Each row in the chart represents two rows worked (one RS row and one WS row) to create one garter stitch ridge. The colour to be worked on each row is determined by the colour of the first st in the first column on the chart.

First, work the RS row reading the chart from right to left. Then, turn your work and work the return WS row with the same colour, reading the chart from left to right.

On each row, knit all sts shown in the colour you are using, and slip all sts shown in the other colour.

Always slip sts purlwise and carry the yarn across the back of the work (with yarn at the back of the st on RS rows, and with yarn in front of the st on WS rows). Do not cut off the yarn at the end of WS rows. Drop the yarn just used and pick up the new yarn ready to work the next row.

FINISHING

STRANDED COLOURWORK

When working with multiple colours in a row, the yarn not being used is carried along the back of the work until it is needed again. This leaves a short strand, or length, of yarn across the back of the work. When you change colour, simply let the first colour hang down at the back of the work until needed again and pick up the new colour to work the next stitch. Try not to pull too tightly when changing colours as this can pucker the stitches and affect your overall gauge (tension). When working stranded colourwork it is important to be consistent with the position of the yarns when switching colours.

The way yarns are held while stranding will affect which yarn shows more dominantly in the knitted fabric, called yarn dominance. For patterns where there is a distinct pattern on a background, this can help make the pattern colour stand out against the background. While working the chart, hold the background colour in your right hand, and the pattern colour in your left hand for yarn dominance.

WEAVING IN ENDS

Thread the yarn end through a tapestry needle and secure it on the wrong side of the work by passing the needle through the 'bumps' of approximately 8 to 10 stitches, changing direction about halfway along. You can work horizontally or diagonally. If possible, keep the tail within the same colour stitches to avoid it showing through. Trim any excess yarn.

BLOCKING

Always check the ball band for any yarn care instructions. Blocking will help smooth out your gauge (tension) and make sure you have straight edges when sewing together your completed tiles for larger projects.

To wet block, soak your tile in a basin filled with lukewarm water and a small amount of wool wash or a mild shampoo. Do not agitate or you risk felting the fabric. Lift the tile carefully, and place the tile on a towel then gently squeeze out the excess water without wringing the fabric. Lay the tile on a flat surface and use rust-proof pins to shape and pin out to the final measurements. Leave in place until completely dry.

MATTRESS STITCH

With right sides of both pieces facing you, secure yarn at the bottom of one piece. Pass the needle to the opposite piece and insert the needle though one stitch, passing under the bar between the V of the stitch. Pull the yarn through gently and over the seam, as if lacing a shoelace, but do not pull the stitch tight. *Insert the needle into the corresponding stitch on the opposite side, going under two bars between Vs of stitches. Repeat from * until you have reached the last stitch, pulling to tighten only after every few stitches or so, adjusting the tension to match the surrounding fabric. At the end of the seam, cut and secure the yarn.

WHIP STITCH

Whip stitch seams create a line of diagonal stitches along the seamed edge. You can hold the pieces together with right sides or wrong sides facing, depending on the effect you prefer. Using a tapestry needle, anchor a stitch at the starting corner. For each stitch bring the needle up through both layers of fabric from the bottom straight to the top of the fabric, then bring the yarn up and over the seam at a slight diagonal ready to pierce into the bottom of the fabric at a slight diagonal, with the stitch forming over the seam edge. Work evenly and with an even tension, keeping the stitches an equal distance apart. At the end of the seam, cut and secure the yarn.

THE DESIGNERS

The publisher would like to thank all of the designers whose patterns and projects appear in this book.

KAROLINA ADAMCZYK
Instagram: @kroopa.knits
Website: kroopaknits.pl

ANNIKEN ALLIS
Instagram: @yarnaddictanni
Website: yarnaddict.co.uk

ANNAPLEXIS
Instagram: @annaplexis.knits
Website: annaplexis.eu

HELEN BIRCH
Instagram: @helen_elizabeth_b

JOANNE FOWLER
Instagram: @madewithloveandfibres
Website: madewithloveandfibres.com

ASHLEY GIBBONS
Instagram: @ashley.the.happy.hooker
Website: ashleythehappyhooker.com

JACQUI GOULBOURN
Instagram: @catkitbob_crochet
Website: catkitbob.com

DANIELLE HOLKE
Instagram: @knithacker
Website: knithacker.com

ANNI HOWARD
Instagram: @annidomino
Website: annihoward.com

CARMEN JORISSEN
Instagram: @newleafdesigns.nl
Website: newleafdesigns.nl

LILY LANGMAN
Instagram: @lilyknitsincumbria

LISA MCFETRIDGE
Instagram: @idlehandsknits

ANNA NIKIPIROWICZ
Instagram: @annanikipirowicz
Website: moochka.co.uk

AZMIYA PADAVIA
Instagram: @rose_trotteuse

SUZY RAI
Instagram: @suzyraiknits

LYNNE ROWE
Instagram: @the_woolnest
Website: knitcrochetcreate.com

ARELLA SEATON
Instagram: @arellaseatondesign
Website: arellaseatondesign.com

SYLVIA WATTS-CHERRY
Instagram: @withcherriesontoptoo
Website: withcherriesontop.com

ASHLEIGH WEMPE
Instagram: @ashleighwempe
Website: ashleighwempe.com

KARIE WESTERMANN
Website: kariebookish.net

INDEX

A DAVID AND CHARLES BOOK
© David and Charles, Ltd 2024

David and Charles is an imprint of David and Charles, Ltd
Suite A, Tourism House, Pynes Hill, Exeter, EX2 5WS

Text and Designs © David and Charles, Ltd 2024
Layout and Photography © David and Charles, Ltd 2024

First published in the UK and USA in 2024

A catalogue record for this book is available from the
British Library.

ISBN-13: 9781446310205 paperback
ISBN-13: 9781446310212 EPUB
ISBN-13: 9781446310229 PDF

This book has been printed on paper from approved suppliers
and made from pulp from sustainable sources.

Printed in China through Asia Pacific Offset for:
David and Charles, Ltd
Suite A, Tourism House, Pynes Hill, Exeter, EX2 5WS

10 9 8 7 6 5 4 3 2 1

Publishing Director: Ame Verso
Senior Commissioning Editor: Sarah Callard
Managing Editor: Jeni Chown
Technical Edit and Charts: Tricia Gilbert
Head of Design: Anna Wade
Designer: Blanche Williams
Pre-press Designer: Susan Reansbury
Illustrations: Kuo Kang Chen
Photography: Jason Jenkins
Art Direction: Laura Woussen
Production Manager: Beverley Richardson

David and Charles publishes high-quality books on
a wide range of subjects. For more information visit
www.davidandcharles.com.

Share your makes with us on social media using #dandcbooks
and follow us on Facebook and Instagram by searching
for @dandcbooks.

Layout of the digital edition of this book may vary depending
on reader hardware and display settings.